No Surprises
Harmonizing Risk and Reward in Volunteer Management
4th Edition

by Melanie L. Herman,
Peggy M. Jackson and
Barbara B. Oliver

Copyright © 2006
by the Nonprofit Risk Management Center

All Rights Reserved.

ISBN 1-893210-20-0

**Nonprofit
Risk Management
Center**

About the Nonprofit Risk Management Center

The Nonprofit Risk Management Center is dedicated to helping community-serving nonprofits prevent harm, conserve resources, preserve assets, and free up resources for mission-critical activities. The Center provides technical assistance on risk management, liability, and insurance matters; publishes easy-to-use written materials; designs and delivers workshops and conferences; and offers competitively priced consulting services.

The Center is an independent nonprofit organization that doesn't sell insurance or endorse specific insurance providers. For more information on the products and services available from the Center, call (202) 785-3891 or visit our Web site at **www.nonprofitrisk.org**.

Nonprofit Risk Management Center
1130 Seventeenth Street, NW
Suite 210
Washington, DC 20036
(202) 785-3891
Fax: (202) 296-0349
www.nonprofitrisk.org

Staff

Sheryl Augustine, *Customer Service Representative*
Melanie L. Herman, *Executive Director*
Barbara B. Oliver, *Director of Communications*
John C. Patterson, *Senior Program Director*

George L. Head, Ph.D., *Special Advisor*

This publication is designed to provide accurate and authoritative information in regard to the subject matter covered. It is distributed with the understanding that the publisher is not engaged in rendering legal, accounting, or other professional service. If legal advice or other expert assistance is required, the services of a competent professional should be sought. From a Declaration of Principles jointly adopted by a Committee of the American Bar Association and a Committee of Publishers.

Table of Contents

Introduction

L ife is often full of surprises—good and bad. If you manage
volunteer resources, or serve as a volunteer for a nonprofit,
chances are you have had your share. You know that the
unpredictable and the unforeseen can be, at best, a distraction
that can divert time, energy and vital resources away from your
mission. At worse, a bad surprise could be devastating to your
nonprofit.

The essential principles of risk management are simple and
straightforward. Risk is the potential for events to differ from
what you expect. Risk management is the ongoing process of
assessing that potential deviation and finding ways to
minimize the chance that bad surprises will occur and increase
the chance of good surprises. Risk management is also about
the steps your nonprofit takes to minimize the effect of a loss
or an unforeseen event that couldn't be prevented.

Risk management isn't something that you do once and
forget about. Nor is it a plan in an attractive binder suitable for
shelving. Rather risk management is an approach to problem
solving. Because the least expensive and most morally
defensible route is to prevent losses before they occur, this book
will focus on prevention as the primary risk control strategy.

Although avoiding legal liability and purchasing adequate
insurance are important topics, the best way to avoid being
sued or needing to file an insurance claim is to prevent harm
from occurring in the first place.

To help you increase your comfort with risk taking and your responsibility for managing risk, this book provides both general and specific guidance. Although this book is filled with useful information and ideas, it's a quick start, *not* a complete risk management guide. To manage your risks effectively, you will need to refer to other materials and experts. The "Resources" section of this book can point you in the right direction.

Because the universe of risks is virtually infinite, getting started with risk management can seem overwhelming. You may even feel that you are diverting precious time away from your "real" work to engage in speculation about what may never occur. One of the ironies of effective risk management is that it's impossible to document the losses you avoided due to effective precautions. Yet consider how a serious accident or incident could affect and impair your organization. True, you can purchase insurance to replace property and equipment, but no amount of money can completely compensate a person who is injured nor can it repair either a demoralized volunteer corps or serious damage to your organization's reputation.

It's About Mission

If you want to understand what risk management is all about, start by reviewing your organization's mission statement. Most nonprofits strive to make a difference in a very positive way, by helping people, removing barriers, improving the environment, extending a hand to those in need and making the world a better place. Whatever your mission, it certainly doesn't involve causing injury or harm to those whom you are dedicated to serving. Likewise, other legal mishaps or missteps may not cause direct harm but can divert resources away from service delivery. Like the physician's Hippocratic oath, the risk manager's cry is "First, do no harm." The safety of your volunteers, service recipients and staff should always be your first priority.

Your volunteers provide a few more reasons to embrace risk management. Do current volunteers worry about injuries? Are potential board members discouraged by fear of lawsuits from serving on your board? Fortunately volunteers are rarely injured and even less often sued, but it does happen. Risk management gives *you* the tools to protect your volunteers and gives *them* the ability to approach their direct service or leadership roles with confidence.

An important goal of risk management is to improve performance by acknowledging and managing risks. It puts you, not the risk, in charge. Contrary to common belief, risk management isn't just about buying insurance. It isn't just about avoiding lawsuits. It *is* about protecting and conserving your organization's resources and providing goods and services sensibly. Risk management frees your organization to pursue its mission by allowing your organization to take more—not less —risk. The difference is that your approach to risk can be structured and calculated rather than haphazard.

As you read this book, keep your mission statement and your volunteers in mind. Consider your volunteers and the community you serve when deciding which precautions to take. Always think about how new risk management strategies will be perceived and received by your volunteers before finalizing these strategies.

Nonprofits face special risk management challenges. Many large corporations and government agencies have the resources to hire their own full-time professional risk managers. A handful of nonprofits have their own risk managers, too. But for the majority of the nation's 1.8 million nonprofits, the role of risk manager is carried out by an individual who has many other responsibilities. In other cases, risk management is a shared responsibility. If adding risk management to a single staff member's job description won't work in your nonprofit, consider getting everyone—the paid and volunteer staff, even your service recipients and board members—thinking like risk managers. Give your nonprofit a risk management culture and make "Safety First" your motto.

If you have questions as you are going through this book, or as you develop risk management strategies for your volunteer program, please contact the Nonprofit Risk Management Center by e-mail (info@nonprofitrisk.org) on the Web (www.nonprofitrisk.org under *Tools*) or by phone — (202) 785-3891. We are here to help.

Chapter 1
Volunteer Organizations Are Natural Risk Takers

V olunteer programs and organizations that rely principally on volunteers have a number of characteristics in common, including:

❑ faith in a cause or the need to provide services to a community;

❑ limitless creativity and the will to make things happen;

❑ copious amounts of enthusiasm;

❑ diverse talents and expertise congregating around a common goal or mission; and

❑ limited resources to spend on the latest management technique or strategy.

And one more thing:

❑ the willingness to take risk to achieve a compelling mission.

Volunteer programs take risks by working with underserved members of a community. They refuse to say, "It can't be done" when a large group of people require emergency assistance in the aftermath of a disaster. They embrace risk when the potential reward is the opportunity to improve the quality of life in a community. And they never shy away from finding a way to serve client groups that government is unable to serve efficiently or the private sector can't serve profitably.

Effective volunteer programs can't operate without taking risks. The only way volunteer programs can avoid risk altogether is to pack up and close down.

Believing that risk management is simply avoiding risk isn't only wrong; it's dangerous. Volunteer programs that embrace *risk* may inadvertently shy away from *risk management*, if they fear that once they dip a foot in the water, the entire mission of the organization will be called into question. Volunteer program leaders may fear that seminal programs will be shut down or dramatically curtailed, despite substantial proof that the programs are making a difference.

What is risk management in the dynamic context of a volunteer organization? The **Risk Management Process** is a series of five steps. The process enables an organization, working through a team of people, to methodically identify the priority risks facing the organization and establish a plan for taking action on those risks. Before getting to strategy, the team looks at the environment or context in which the organization operates. The team then moves to risk identification and prioritization. The latter is simply a way of determining where to begin or put the emphasis.

After priorities have been selected, the team determines what it will do about the organization's priority risks. In most cases the strategies selected by the team will involve changing certain activities in small ways to make them safer for the nonprofit and its constituencies—such as clients, volunteers, staff, donors and members of the general public. If the risk is too great and a particular activity isn't essential to accomplish the organization's mission, the preferred action will be to avoid the risk by forgoing the activity altogether.

In certain instances there may be the opportunity to manage a risk by contracting with another organization that is willing to assume responsibility if undesired events occur. And sometimes, after giving the risk due consideration, the team will decide to do nothing about it. Maybe it's because the risk is so remote and others require immediate attention. Maybe it's because the organization must make resource allocation decisions and there simply isn't enough money, people or time to go around. Or maybe it's because the only things to do are simply out of the reach of the organization. That's risk management in a nutshell—nothing more.

Risk Management Process

establish the context

acknowledge & identify risk

evaluate and prioritize risk

implement risk management techniques

monitor and update the program

Is the discipline of risk management in a volunteer organization the same as the discipline of risk management in a large manufacturing organization? Yes, and no. Yes, in that the same risk management process employed by professionals with certificates, degrees and other risk management credentials can be applied in the smallest nonprofit organization, even an all-volunteer agency. No, in that in a volunteer program *a risk management effort must be created on a scale that is consistent with the organization's operations and resources,* or chance winding up at as a dust-covered reminder of someone's good intentions.

Back to the volunteer program, where a group of dedicated, cause-oriented, compassionate individuals have come together to address a critical need. Volunteers are usually people who work 40+ hour weeks and bring unlimited enthusiasm but limited time to a nonprofit. Volunteers want their contributions to be meaningful and bear fruit for the intended recipients of those services.

Does a full-blown risk management program employing the traditional five-part risk management process make sense for all-volunteer or principally volunteer organizations? It can certainly be adapted to meet the needs and circumstances facing a small or volunteer organization. For example, instead of relying on a full-time professional risk manager to champion safety and risk management activities, the small organization may assemble a volunteer committee dubbed the "risk management committee" or "risk management task force."

Here's an alternative approach that may be less likely to get a volunteer organization bogged down in process, and back to building homes for low-income families, or providing after-school recreational programs for latchkey kids, or providing a safe place to live and counseling for victims of domestic violence. Here's how it works.

Step 1

First, identify the key activities, programs and services provided by your volunteer program and your expectations for that activity or program. For a volunteer program established to provide home repair services for low-income seniors on one day every year, the activities of the organization might boil down to the following simple list:

❑ *Parameters for volunteer service*—developing position descriptions for the work volunteers will be doing. Expectation: the nonprofit will have a clear understanding of the skills it requires before it begins recruiting volunteers.

❑ *Volunteer recruitment*—finding people willing to devote one Saturday in May to performing home repair and gardening tasks. Expectation: more than 150 folks will volunteer for the 125 volunteer slots the nonprofit needs to fill for this year's Home Repair Day.

❑ *Volunteer training*—outfitting volunteers with the information and tools they need to provide meaningful assistance during the annual Home Repair Day. Expectation: that volunteers will be enthusiastic and attentive as we present program rules and safety information, and that all volunteers will come equipped with a willingness to ask questions if they are uncertain about an assignment.

❑ *Deployment/assignment to client homes*—matching volunteers with elderly residents requesting help and those identified by the Area Agency on Aging as needing help. Expectation: that volunteers will willingly accept the matches made by the director of volunteers and have little or no difficulty reaching their assignment sites.

❑ *Provide home repair*—coordinating the work of home helpers who will be weeding gardens; tidying attics, basements and garages; fixing screen doors and storm windows; painting railings; and installing grab rails, handrails, nonskid floor mats, etc. Expectation: that volunteers will exercise care in providing home help to senior clients, and that clients will be more than satisfied with the work performed during the Home Repair Day.

Step 2

Next, use an existing group of program leaders, such as the board of directors, veteran volunteers, finance committee or another small group, to ask and answer the following questions:

❑ *What could go wrong?* What surprises could occur in each of the five key tasks described above?

❑ *What will we do to prevent these things from going wrong?* Armed with our ability to predict the kinds of things that could go wrong, what reasonable steps could we take to eliminate those surprises? Answers might revolve around what the organization can adjust in the areas of position design, recruitment, screening, training and supervising volunteers.

❏ *What will we do if something does go wrong?* What if our attempts to prevent harm fail, and something goes wrong anyway? Will the people on site know what to do? What will the organization do, if anything?

❏ *How will we pay for harm?* Do the potential "surprises" have a price tag? What might it cost if a volunteer damages a client's property? Who should pay for medical expenses if a volunteer gets hurt? What if the program is sued? What if the volunteer doesn't have medical insurance? Do either the volunteers or the volunteer program have adequate insurance coverage or funds on hand to pay for harm?

The ultimate effectiveness of the ideas and strategies coming from the team discussion depends on whether:

■ the ideas are inherently practical and take into account the existing financial and human resources of the volunteer program.

■ the strategies can be implemented without jeopardizing the community-serving mission of the organization. For example, if a proposed strategy for managing the risks inherent in mentoring is to limit the program to after-school tutoring in the library, that's fine, if the mission is to provide tutoring. But, if the organization was established to provide community-based mentoring for children, then the risk management strategy has unwittingly altered the very nature of the program.

■ the strategies result in maximum time and resources being available for community-serving work. If the strategy consumes 50 percent of volunteer time to implement, then a great deal less time is available to repair the homes of low-income seniors or mentor children.

- the strategies are reasonable given the time constraints at hand. A process for screening vacation Bible-school teachers that takes the entire summer to complete isn't a good risk management strategy.

There's lots of goods news about volunteer risk management, including:

- *Everyone's doing it.* Whether you know it or not, your volunteer program probably has a lot of great risk management strategies in place. You may call these strategies "common sense," or "safety measures" or simply "good management." Whatever the label, these decisions and strategies put your program on a solid footing and in many respects enable your volunteer program to stride confidently toward its mission.

- *Do what you can, when you can.* Risk management in volunteer programs often involves taking small steps, as soon as practically possible. Don't be intimidated by what larger organizations are doing. Remember that your risk management program should reflect the resources available to your organization.

- *Use risk management to bolster volunteer recruitment.* Everyone wants to work and volunteer in a safe environment. As your program focuses additional attention on risk management, your safety activities will become points of pride for the program.

Conclusion

Volunteer risk management is within the reach of every nonprofit that engages volunteers. A risk management program should appropriately reflect the mission of the organization and the resources at its disposal. In Chapter 2, we'll present a list of critical do's and don'ts for volunteer risk management. Then, in Chapter 3, we'll address some of the common areas of risk facing volunteer programs, which will help you avoid the potholes and pitfalls other groups have encountered.

Chapter 2
10 Strategies for Managing Volunteer Service Risks

1. **Apply liberal doses of common sense**—It's not unusual for someone leaving a workshop on nonprofit risk management to remark, "A lot of what we heard today was about using common sense." But like sunscreen, common sense must be applied liberally in order for it to be effective as a risk management tool.

2. **Involve your volunteers**—In an all-volunteer program, the director of volunteers wouldn't dream of achieving the organization's mission without volunteers, nor should the risk management point person consider implementing risk management strategies without their input. While the director of volunteers may be keenly aware of the risks in a screening process, she may not be aware that Home Helper Day volunteers are using rusty power tools and climbing up on peaked roofs to fulfill their assignments. The participants in the program, on the other hand, will be aware of activities that require an injection of safety or additional safety precautions.

3. **Provide explicit direction**—Volunteers want to succeed. And, generally speaking, they want to meet the high standards set by your volunteer program. To help them do so, you need to provide explicit direction about what you expect and what is required to volunteer in your program. You may expect an ongoing commitment of five hours per week, or a minimum level of weekly contact between a

volunteer mentor and his or her mentee. You may require that volunteers attend a safety briefing before the Home Helper Day or submit regular, detailed written reports on their work with a literacy client. And you need to tell them what's forbidden—even when it's a topic that you may be uncomfortable discussing with a group of relative strangers or something that "should be obvious." These might include your program's prohibition against volunteers engaging in sexual relationships with any client, and your prohibition against transporting clients in personal vehicles or inviting clients to a volunteer's home.

4. **Praise and punish**—Every director of volunteers knows the importance of recognizing the outstanding performance and valued contributions of a volunteer. There are terrific publications and online resources available containing suggestions that range from free and simple to expensive and elaborate, and you'll get a lot of ideas from your volunteers. From volunteer recognition banquets to nominating someone for a presidential award, it's vital that a volunteer program praise hard work and let volunteers know their efforts are appreciated. It's equally important to let volunteers know when their performance has fallen below your standards, when they have done something prohibited by your program or failed to fulfill your organization's requirements. It's doubly important, and a lot more difficult, to remove volunteers whose continued participation poses too great a risk to the health and safety of the organization, its clients or other volunteers. From time-to-time in every volunteer program's lifetime, firing offenses can't be avoided and must be taken care of if the mission of the program is worth preserving.

5. **Don't assume**—Just as you can't assume new volunteers are familiar with the safe operation of a chain saw before you send them out to cut fallen logs, you can't make assumptions about the organizations with which your volunteer program eagerly partners. Collaboration is the name of the game for 21st century nonprofits. Many nonprofits prefer not to "go it alone." And others simply

don't have the resources to meet critical client needs without partnerships and collaborations. Volunteer programs partner with other informal programs, well-established nonprofits, government agencies and private businesses. And, for the most part, these collaborations expand services, increase your pool of volunteers and generate resources that weren't available when you were acting alone. But when collaborations end in controversy and disappointment they consume, rather than generate, resources for the volunteer program. One of the most common mistakes in collaboration is assuming that "the other guy took care of it." A volunteer program should never assume that its partner has taken care of details, such as obtaining appropriate insurance to pre-screening the volunteers an organization sends your way. You need to determine who's done what and what open items need to be handled and by whom.

6. **Establish policies and follow through**—Policies and procedures are often at the heart of preventing surprises in a volunteer program. As you develop policies that meet the needs of your organization, make sure that they are communicated to all personnel. Doing so will prevent surprise on the part of the unwitting or unaware volunteer. Policies are critical for a number of reasons. They:

❏ *establish a standard for behavior and a common body of knowledge.* Clear rules increase the likelihood that all people will understand their responsibilities and do what they are supposed to do.

❏ *support necessary requirements.* For example, if official policy requires that every potential mentor participates in two in-person interviews, when a board member's brother requests a waiver of the interview requirement, you can tell him "No, " because your "policy requires interviews." Written policies are invaluable when you need to discipline or terminate a volunteer or employee. They provide equity for all staff—paid and volunteer—and decrease the perception of subjectivity or favoritism.

- *provide a valuable orientation and training tool for volunteers, employees, board members and clients.* People want to succeed. Knowing how to do things and knowing what is expected helps to reinforce appropriate and safe actions.

- *help ensure operational consistency.* Written instructions decrease the risks of mistakes and downtime when the backup to a key volunteer is asked to "fill-in" on a temporary basis.

- *demonstrate diligence if the organization or its volunteers are sued.* For example, a written contractor selection policy that is carefully and faithfully applied may convince a judge or jury that the organization didn't act negligently in selecting a bus company to transport campers.

Established, written policies are rendered useless when an organization or its senior managers don't follow them. It's critical that every volunteer program makes a commitment to adhere to its established policies and update them as needed.

- *Ensure widespread communication*—Distribute your written policies to target groups. Many nonprofits have developed volunteer handbooks as a way to capture core policies in a single location. Some groups give paid and volunteer staff time to read the manual and require that they initial each page. Others also post these policies on a Web site. Make sure you provide each group an opportunity to ask questions.

- *Don't make promises you can't honor*—A risk management program is doomed when it's based on lofty promises and ignored policies. Make sure that your nonprofit can live with and practice the policies it embraces.

- *Monitor policy implementation and revise policies that aren't working*—Solicit volunteers' feedback about whether key policies are effective. Involve those who complain in updating and revising policies.

❏ *Get help*—It's always a good idea to obtain assistance from outside professionals when you're developing or updating key volunteer management policies. Having an independent legal advisor review policies before you implement them is an excellent risk management strategy.

7. **Empower the board to meet its legal duties**—One of the most important contributions that a nonprofit board makes to an organization's overall risk management effort is to manage its own affairs properly. Effective governance includes conducting board activities in accordance with the nonprofit's governing documents and ensuring compliance with various regulations. The board's actions should model its commitment to excellent management, including risk management. When the board takes its responsibilities seriously, others will follow their lead. A nonprofit board has specific legal duties of care, loyalty and obedience. The public, the nonprofit's constituencies, and state and federal governments all have a stake in the proper management of a nonprofit.

❏ The *duty of care* asks a director to be reasonably informed, participate in decisions, and to act in good faith and with the care of an ordinarily prudent person in similar circumstances. Ways to assess the board's commitment include asking if board members participate actively in decisions, attend meetings, use independent judgment, and seek reliable information in order to make informed decisions.

❏ The *duty of loyalty* requires that a board member put the interests of the organization first, ahead of any personal interest or the interest of another party or entity. Loyalty issues usually arise from actual or perceived conflicts of interest, appropriation of a corporate opportunity (a member engages in a transaction that may be of interest to the organization), and breaches of confidentiality. Every nonprofit should have policies on conflicts of interest and confidentiality.

❑ The *duty of obedience* requires the board to act in accordance with the nonprofit's mission and all applicable laws and regulations. A common allegation of board malfeasance is that the board isn't staying true to the organization's mission and purpose. Many external entities regulate and monitor nonprofits closely to ensure that they maintain their charitable functions.

Meeting a board's legal duties isn't easy. These critical volunteers must be committed to being effective board members. The organization can enhance the board's ability to act appropriately by providing its members with information and guidance. Many nonprofits provide a manual to board members to assure that they receive key documents and information on the organization's history, structure and activities. Another tool is a board orientation program to up date new board members quickly. Board minutes also serve to both inform members and to document the board's actions. These and other activities will help a board meet its responsibilities. Some of the questions every nonprofit board should ask itself include:

❑ Does the board keep thorough, accurate records? Do the board meeting minutes document the decisions made, including a summary of the major points of discussion? Are dissenting votes recorded?

❑ Does the board have a manual and operating procedures?

❑ Does the board explore options before arriving at a decision?

❑ Are attendance policies in place and enforced for board members who fail to participate?

❑ Do board members stay informed about the nonprofit's activities? Are background materials provided in advance of each meeting? Do board members ask questions and seek clarification on matters before them?

❑ Does the board have a conflict of interest policy? Is the policy followed?

8. **Provide guidance on privacy issues**—Access to the Internet and e-mail and attendant litigation have radically changed privacy in the workplace. It's imperative that volunteers who use your equipment as part of their duties understand your applicable rules about technology. They should also be aware that there should be no expectation of privacy while using your equipment and systems, and that all of the nonprofit's equipment is subject to scrutiny and review. This includes messages sent via e-mail and the results of Web searches. Some nonprofits create a reminder message that appears randomly when the staff member or volunteer logs on to the computer. As part of your volunteer training or orientation, define expectations. These might include descriptions of acceptable and unacceptable content of e-mail and Web sites; how to handle errors such as mistakenly forwarding harassing or racially derogative jokes or locating a pornographic Web site while innocently searching a keyword such as "risk"; and consequences when these guidelines are breached.

9. **Use written agreements to spell out requirements**— Written volunteer agreements are one way to maximize your authority in supervising volunteers while limiting your exposure to liability. For example, volunteer agreements: (a) make it easier to determine and account for who is serving as a volunteer in your organization and what their responsibilities are; (b) clearly establish the terms of appointment and reappointment (e.g., for one year, renewable by mutual agreement for an unlimited number of times); (c) remind volunteers that they are serving at the discretion and will of the agency; and (d) establish a sense of accountability of the volunteer to the agency and its rules.

If you decide to use written volunteer agreements as a risk management tool, they should be prepared on your organization's letterhead and contain the following elements:

- ❏ the volunteer's name and contact information (address and phone number);

- ❏ the duration of the appointment (e.g., for one year);

- ❏ the terms of renewal (by a new appointment letter);

- ❏ your volunteer's position title (e.g., Volunteer Fundraiser) and at least a general description of the volunteer's duties or position expectations (e.g., serving on the Fund-raising Committee or assisting with general office duties. Better still, develop a volunteer position description and attach it to the appointment letter);

- ❏ the department and/or supervisor to whom the volunteer will report;

- ❏ a statement that the volunteer has received, read and will comply with your organization's purposes, policies and rules, including your organization's:

  - ➤ mission statement

  - ➤ nondiscrimination policy

  - ➤ anti-harassment policy

  - ➤ policy that the organization's co-workers and clients are to be treated with respect and courtesy

  - ➤ grievance procedure, and

  - ➤ your organization's office, client and operational procedures and policies (e.g., calendar of days off, use of client logs, telephone/file etiquette).

- ❏ the signature (and date signed) of the executive director or supervisor of volunteers; and

- ❏ the signature (and date signed) of the volunteer.

10. **Make risk management everyone's responsibility—**
Basic proactive do's and don'ts are learned from childhood:
Brush your teeth. Wash your face. Look both ways when
you cross the street. Hot! Don't touch. Just as all members
of a household are educated and expected to manage their
own risks, you'll want each volunteer in your organization
to be aware and practice risk management. Infuse your
"corporate" culture with safe practices in the treatment of
service recipients, each other and the public.

Safety Checklist

1. Check lighting in stairways, entrances, emergency exits, parking areas
    and individual work areas.

2. Make sure exits are easily accessible and clearly marked. Can visitors
    find their way out in a smoke-filled hallway?

3. Are hazardous materials (such as paint, gasoline and toner) and cleaning
    supplies (such as bleach and ammonia) clearly marked and properly
    stored? Have special disposal arrangements been made and publicized?

4. Are workstations properly aligned to prevent eye, back, neck, shoulder
    and wrist strain?

5. Do volunteers who drive while performing their duties follow defensive
    driving practices? This would include everyone in the vehicle wearing
    seatbelts; not driving when sleepy, taking medication that causes
    drowsiness or after drinking alcohol; using reverse gear as little as
    possible; and driving with headlights on.

6. Are volunteers trained to look for and remedy slip or trip conditions on
    steps and floors? These would be spills, loose rugs, slick paper, pencils
    or extension cords.

Conclusion

Follow the critical do's and don'ts outlined in this chapter to create a sound foundation for managing risk in your nonprofit organization. Yes, the exercise will require an investment of time and thought, but the results will pay off for your organization and your volunteer staff. Chapter 3 addresses some of the common areas of risk facing volunteer programs. Continue on to learn how to avoid the challenges other groups have had to face and conquer.

Chapter 3
Volunteers Seek Challenge and Fulfillment

Volunteers in the United States reflect the national profile: multi-ethnic, male and female, child through senior citizen with skills from manual labor through computer programmer to rocket scientist. Commitments range from a half-day chaperoning a school trip through periodic seasonal service to full-time volunteering in the Peace Corps. Those nonprofits that have successful volunteer programs find they've had to re-evaluate their needs in light of the range of time commitments people are able to give and the higher skills they are able to provide. Successful nonprofits have been able to structure volunteer opportunities to accommodate what the volunteer workforce has to offer.

Susan J. Ellis refers to this "range or scope of activities" as "scale of service intensity." In an article in *The NonProfit Times*, Sept. 1, 2001, she lists the 10 levels of commitment as:

1. a public extension of helping oneself (chaperoning son's class trip, ushering at daughter's play);

2. one-time, help-for-a-day projects (clean-ups, drives);

3. goal-oriented, short-term projects that end when the goal is achieved (political campaigns, building a playground);

4. periodic or seasonal service (clean-ups, planting or harvesting, summer reading);

5. on-call service (sign language interpreting, substituting for absent volunteer);

6. ongoing service scheduled at the volunteer's convenience, off site (virtual volunteering, translating documents);

7. regularly scheduled, ongoing participation—administrative or technical services;

8. regularly scheduled, ongoing participation—governance;

9. regularly scheduled, ongoing participation—direct service to client or consumers; and

10. full-time volunteering (disaster relief, Peace Corps).

The risks involved with the different "levels of intensity" vary. As you plan for "no surprises," you'll use the same principles, but adjust them to meet the needs of protecting 1) a one-time, one-day volunteer at your fund-raising event 2) a full-time volunteer, and 3) your nonprofit.

Demographics

The growing diversity of the volunteer workforce brings with it challenges to make programs and orientations culturally and age sensitive and meaningful to participants. The growing number of senior and youth volunteers provide examples of the changing volunteer work force. Expectations and requirements need to be explained in a way that is understood and accepted by all. It's more important than ever to provide a thorough orientation program for new volunteers and emphasize your high expectations with respect to their contributions and performance. Diversity training and sensitivity take a more important role, particularly in those programs that have experienced an influx of new volunteers and/or have a long-standing core of paid and volunteer staff. Ideally, the organization's paid and volunteer staffs have gender, ethnic and/or community ties to the organization's client base.

Equally important are volunteer screening and verifying the validity of documents—driver's licenses for those positions that require driving, and professional licenses—before the volunteer can begin his or her assignment. Another aspect of the screening process is ensuring that the volunteer and the assignment are a good "match." Some volunteers want assignments in the same arenas as their professions; others want to work in areas completely different from the type of work that they are paid to do. It's important to determine assignment preferences and, whenever possible, honor the volunteer's inclinations, while at the same time meeting the needs of your organization and its clients.

Duration of Commitment

The short-term, temporary aspect of volunteer assignments again emphasizes the significance of a thorough orientation. The organization's expectations in terms of performance, behavior, organizational norms and public relations need to be emphasized. If volunteers will have unsupervised access to vulnerable clients, they should be subject to a rigorous (versus basic) screening process.

Special events or short-term projects may have numerous volunteers working at one time, some who just walk in off the street. There is virtually no time for screening or orientation or obtaining necessary data for volunteer records. This type of scenario needs to be recognized and considered during the planning phase of the event. The nonprofit may have to risk turning away volunteers, rather than losing control of the staffing of an event.

Access to client information should be carefully monitored. Sensitive material such as financial records, proprietary documents and client records should be secured, and access limited to individuals who have been thoroughly screened—paid and volunteer staff—and need the information to perform their duties.

Affiliation

Before a decision is made to partner with a community group or corporation on any volunteer project, the nonprofit needs to carefully consider the implications of associating with the group. Would this type of collaboration harm the image of the nonprofit, or call into question the commitment of the nonprofit to its mission or values?

In any form of collaboration with an outside group, such issues as insurance, transportation, supervision and accountability need to be settled in advance and committed to in writing. It's also important to establish accountability for screening and placing volunteers who are work with a nonprofit as part of a larger program, such as community service in academic settings. But risk management never ends with the completion of a screening process. The staff and students at an elementary school learned a frightening lesson about the importance of supervision. A student from a prestigious university who had volunteered to teach safety classes at the school was arrested for soliciting a sexual encounter with a 10-year-old girl via an e-mail address he'd gotten while teaching at the school. The child's parents intercepted the e-mail and turned the matter over to police who set up a sting operation.

Skills

The advanced skills of today's volunteer workers have the potential to both enhance and diminish volunteer programs. Properly managed and supervised, the skills volunteers bring to the organization can benefit the overall program. The same skills, as we saw in the case of the college student who used the e-mail to attempt to meet and assault a young student, can cause great harm to clients and permanently damage the reputation of an organization or program.

Managers and program directors need to consider the types of skills needed to facilitate success. They also need to determine how those individuals who possess the skills can be acclimated to the program, supervised and, if necessary, redirected to ensure that the services they provide match the project's needs. This matchmaking is particularly important when working with groups.

Expectations

Volunteers see their assignments as opportunities to fulfill personal interests, use special skills, develop or refine emerging skills and to network. Volunteers who have been recently laid off or are in between jobs, and those recently retired seek networking opportunities to stay in touch with their areas of expertise. These volunteers have much to offer, and the nonprofit has much to offer them in return. Social events, in addition to the social exchanges during the volunteer assignment, could provide additional opportunities for networking and the potential to recruit other volunteers, if participants are invited to bring a friend.

Expectations of volunteers and the organization need to be clear and presented openly. When working with organizations such as academic institutions, corporations and community groups, expectations need to be particularly clear and committed to in writing. These steps benefit the volunteer program, as well as the organization providing volunteers. It's particularly important to ensure that expectations from both sides are presented. Vague or general comments such as, "The XYZ Corporation wants its staff to work with the ABC Nonprofit to help feed needy people and contribute to the community" don't describe specific issues such as liability, insurance, public relations, supervision or specifics of the assignment.

Rewards

Thanking and rewarding volunteers are important means of recognizing their contributions, reinforcing their successes and retaining their services. Awards should be free from any perception of discrimination. If an award is based upon certain criteria, the specifics should be broadcast to all paid and volunteer staff, and the process for nominations must be clearly stated. It's important to be aware that even a perception of bias will diminish the credibility of the awards process, and can also result in the loss of valuable volunteers—who also might be major donors.

Program Design

Volunteer programs and projects need to be designed to address organizational goals and objectives, and the nonprofit's focus and desired outcomes should be clear to all volunteer staff. Performance objectives for either an individual or a group must be clearly stated and managed. The accountable staff member—whether paid or volunteer—should closely supervise the program and hold subordinate supervisors accountable for volunteer activities.

Keep in mind that some of your volunteers may not be suitable as caregivers for certain client groups. Your screening process should take into consideration the special needs of your client population and strive to match volunteers to the programs for which they are best suited.

Myths About Managing Volunteer Activities

The more things change, the more they stay the same. In this section we will examine some outdated beliefs about volunteers that remain despite societal and nonprofit sector changes.

❏ *Volunteers can't or shouldn't be supervised, counseled or terminated simply because they are volunteers.*

The belief persists in many circles that a nonprofit shouldn't fire a volunteer—except in instances of severe policy violations or other outrageous conduct. Some organizations treat volunteers with kid gloves, perhaps as a way of compensating for the volunteer's uncompensated status with the organization. Affording volunteers "permanent" or "untouchable" status with an organization is a dangerous practice. Like their paid counterparts, volunteers may be unable or unwilling to fulfill the duties they have been assigned. If reassignment is not possible, or if they violate rules to which they are required to abide, discipline should be imposed. In some cases, performance counseling may prove effective in getting the volunteer to adjust his or her work or attitude. And, from time to time, terminating the nonprofit's relationship with a volunteer is necessary.

❏ *The intent of a volunteer is generally in step with the mission of the nonprofit he or she seeks out for placement.*

This assumption may support an organization's decision not to screen volunteers or require the same conduct imposed on the rest of the organization. Either course is potentially dangerous for the nonprofit, as it misses the opportunity to increase the odds of a successful match between the position available and the prospective volunteer.

❏ *Imposing performance and behavioral expectations on volunteers will send them running out the door of your nonprofit.*

Many nonprofits continue to be reticent about discussing performance and behavioral expectations during the recruitment, screening and supervisory processes. Yet inappropriate volunteer behavior can seriously impair the nonprofit's ability to achieve its mission. In other cases, inappropriate, abusive or difficult behavior on the part of long-standing volunteers may be tolerated because of the volunteer's age, length of tenure with the organization or the belief that volunteers can't be subject to the same workplace controls as the paid staff. In rare cases staff may be expected to tolerate, cover up and get along with a volunteer regardless of the individual's inappropriate behavior or disregard for the nonprofit's standards. This attitude tends to drain a nonprofit's resources when, in fact, the involvement of volunteers is meant to maximize resources. When an organization addresses problematic situations, its staff and volunteers will be relieved and gratified.

Conclusion

Myths about volunteers continue to circulate in the nonprofit sector. While some of these myths contain nuggets of truth, most detract attention from the fact that the vast majority of volunteers seek challenge and fulfillment in their volunteer service roles. And most nonprofits have at their disposal the tools to increase volunteer satisfaction. Along these lines, nonprofits should also examine the way in which volunteers are recruited, screened, trained and supervised. These subjects are explored in the Chapter 4. Remember that every volunteer program, from the smallest to the largest, can take steps to avoid surprise when it comes to providing a meaningful experience for your volunteers and deploying volunteers to improve your community or the quality of life for your clients.

Chapter 4
Integrating Risk Management Into Volunteer Administration

Volunteer administration is the means by which a volunteer program is organized and run. This chapter will examine risk management issues in the administration of volunteer programs. We begin with a description of the volunteer recruitment process, which consists of three principal steps:

Step 1   Develop a Position Description

Step 2   Seek Applicants

Step 3   Screen Applicants

Step 1   Develop a Position Description

Managing the risk that volunteers will work "outside the box" containing your requirements and expectations begins with a detailed description of the responsibilities for the position. This description should be developed long before the first prospective volunteer appears for an interview or arrives to work. Some organizations choose to communicate the terms of the assignment through a volunteer agreement. Another approach is to use a position description, and confirm other details in a letter (similar to an offer letter presented to a prospective employee). The work sheet on the next two pages suggests an approach to developing a position description for a volunteer assignment.

Other categories not included in the sample that an organization would include, if applicable, in a volunteer position description are: appointed by, development opportunities, relationships, age requirement, and benefits provided (i.e., lunch, T-shirt or opportunity to assist a young person achieve academic success).

WORKSHEET & SAMPLE

Volunteer Position Description

Consider using or adapting this worksheet to develop position descriptions for the volunteer positions in your nonprofit.

Sections of the Job Description	Explanation and Example
Purpose:	This section describes the specific purpose of the position in no more than two sentences. If possible, the purpose should be stated in relation to the nonprofit's mission and goals.
Example:	*The position of After-School Tutor supports [Name of Nonprofit]'s educational program for high school students. The tutoring program is designed to help high school students achieve academic success and graduate on time.*
Job Title:	What title has been assigned to the position?
Example:	*After-School Tutor*
Location:	Where will the volunteer work?
Example:	*The After-School Tutoring Program is conducted at the County Library on Main Street.*
Key Responsibilities:	List the position's major duties.
Example:	*The After-School Tutor:*
	(1) works with an assigned high school student to provide assistance in one or more academic subjects;
	(2) assists a student to develop a better understanding of in-class and homework assignments;
	(3) coaches the student in identifying resources to complete assignments;

(4) reviews completed assignments and suggests ways to improve or supplement assignments; and

(5) provides positive feedback on the student's progress and encourages the student's continued focus on academic excellence.

Reports to: Indicate the title of the person to whom the volunteer reports.

Example: *Director of Tutors*

Length of Appointment: Note the time period in which the volunteer will serve, and include restrictions, if applicable.

Example: *The After-School Tutor will serve for the Fall 2007 and Spring 2008 semesters. The tutor is eligible to continue in the 2008/2009 school year with approval from the director of tutors.*

Time Commitment: Indicate the minimum time needed and maximum time permitted.

Example: *The After-School Tutor position requires a minimum commitment of two hours, and no more than four hours per week, for each week that school is in session. In addition, each volunteer must attend a two-hour orientation during the week before the semester begins. The orientation program is held from 3-5 pm each Wednesday.*

Qualifications: List education, experience, knowledge and skills required. If a criminal history record check or other background check will be conducted, it should be indicated here.

Example: *Eligible candidates for the After-School Tutor position include adults over 21 years of age who have earned a bachelor's degree and who pass a criminal history record check.*

Support Provided: List resources that will be available to the volunteer.

Example: *Training for this position will be provided at the two-hour orientation session. In addition, the director of tutors is available on an ongoing basis to answer questions and provide other assistance as needed.*

Step 2   Seek Applicants

The next step in the process is to invite prospective volunteers to complete an application form. The next two pages features a sample volunteer application form.

SAMPLE

Volunteer Application

Application Date _____ Volunteer Position Sought _____

Name _____

Home Address _____

Work Phone _____ Home Phone _____

E-mail Address _____

Highest Level of Education _____

Employment

Provide information on your current employer, if applicable, in the space below:

Position/Title _____

Dates of Employment (starting, ending) _____

Company/Employer _____

Address _____

Would you like us to keep your employer abreast of your volunteer service and achievement?   ❑ Yes   ❑ No

Special training, skills, hobbies _____

Groups, clubs, organizational memberships _____

Please describe your prior volunteer experience (include organization names and dates of service) _____

_____

_____

What experiences have you had that may prepare you to work as a volunteer in the field of [description of field, e.g. domestic violence, child abuse prevention, youth recreation, etc.]? _____

_____

_____

Why do you want to volunteer? [or What do you want to gain from this volunteer experience?] _____

Have you ever been convicted of a crime? (If yes, please explain the nature of the crime and the date of the conviction and disposition.) Conviction of a crime is not an automatic disqualification for volunteer work.

_____

Do you have: a driver's license?   ❏ Yes   ❏ No

Has your driver's license ever been revoked or suspended?   ❏ Yes   ❏ No   ❏ NA

Do you have current car insurance?   ❏ Yes   ❏ No

Does your insurance allow you to transport others?   ❏ Yes   ❏ No

REFERENCES: Please list three people who know you well and can attest to your character, skills and dependability. Include your current or last employer.

[Note: an organization can specify the type of references it requires. This may be particularly important when a volunteer will be performing sensitive work or serving a vulnerable population. For example: Ask a volunteer who will be working with children to provide a reference from a paid staff member at an organization where the volunteer previously served as a coach or tutor.]

Name/Organization   Relationship to You   Phone   Length of relationship

1. _____ _____   _____ _____

2. _____ _____   _____ _____

3. _____ _____   _____ _____

Please read the following carefully before signing this application:

I understand that this is an application for and not a commitment or promise to provide an opportunity to volunteer.

I further understand that by submitting this application I am consenting to the completion of a criminal history records check on myself and that this check will be made from public record sources. I hereby agree to release and hold harmless from liability any person or organization that provides information and the nonprofit named on this application.

I certify that I have and will provide information throughout the selection process, including on this application for a volunteer position and in interviews with [Name of Nonprofit] that is true, correct and complete to the best of my knowledge. I certify that I have and will answer all questions to the best of my ability and that I have not and will not withhold any information that would unfavorably affect my application for a volunteer position. I understand that information contained on my application will be verified by [Name of Nonprofit]. I understand that misrepresentations or omissions may be cause for my immediate rejection as an applicant for a volunteer position with [Name of Nonprofit] or my termination as a volunteer.

Signature _____ Date _____

Step 3   Screen Applicants

Basic to Rigorous Screening Processes

While the screening process in volunteer programs varies based on the needs of each organization, a basic screening process suitable for all positions consists of the following:

- ❑ Application review

- ❑ Face-to-face interview

- ❑ Reference checks

In many volunteer programs there will be positions that pose risks beyond those of the low-risk volunteer role. For those positions, an organization might add tools to its screening process. For example, for a volunteer who will be serving in a supervised educational capacity with vulnerable clients, a program might want to verify the information contained on the application, such as the degrees obtained, past positions and other credentials related to the specific position. In cases where the position involves driving, the program should consider pulling a Department of Motor Vehicles report and comparing the results with the organization's requirements for drivers. These mid-level requirements should be established in advance of the recruitment process and before any DMV records are obtained.

In cases where a position poses a high level of risk, such as when a volunteer will have unsupervised access to a vulnerable client, a rigorous screening process should apply to every applicant who seeks placement in that volunteer position. A rigorous screening process might include everything in a basic or mid-level process plus additional reference checks, a second interview, a home visit, interviews with family members, using training as an extension of the screening process and, perhaps, checking official agency records.

Checklist for Volunteer Screening

❑ Do all volunteer positions have a position description that describes the essential duties and required qualifications of their positions?

❑ Are all applicants for volunteer positions subject to a basic screening process consisting of:

➡ an application,

➡ a face-to-face interview, and

➡ reference checks?

❑ Has the organization assessed each volunteer position by the degree of risk it poses? Is each group of positions subject to an appropriate screening process? The general guideline for screening volunteers is that the more vulnerable the service recipient and the greater the opportunity for violations of trust, the more intensive the screening process must be.

Interviews

The interview is an opportunity to convey expectations, confirm information, gauge emotional responses and probe concerns. An interview is an important part of every screening process. During an interview an applicant may indicate the reasons she or he wants to volunteer with your nonprofit. The organization has an opportunity to identify the skills each prospective volunteer brings that may not be readily apparent on the application. The interviewer needs to allow sufficient time for the discussion to be substantive and for the volunteer to ask any questions that he or she has about the organization. It is a good practice to allow the applicant to talk at least 60 percent of the time—otherwise, it's not an "interview."

Although not required by law, it is good risk management to standardize your interviews in a way that makes it easier to compare applicants for key volunteer positions. One way to do this is to ask every applicant for a particular position the same set of questions. Keep in mind that the questions you ask applicants for a volunteer van driver position will be different

Volunteer Interview Questions

Date of Interview _____ Interviewer_____

Name of Applicant _____

What is your relationship with each of your references?

Why do you want to be a volunteer in this organization?

Have you ever done this type of volunteer work before? Please explain.

What kind of work do you do? What do you like most about your present position?

How would someone close to you describe you? (e.g., friend; spouse; boyfriend or girlfriend; parent; roommate)

What have you done within the last year that has brought you the most satisfaction?

What do you hope to gain from your volunteer experience?

from the set of questions you'll ask applicants seeking placement as mentors to young children. It is up to each volunteer program to design an interview format and set of questions that meet the organization's needs.

It helps to jot down on the application responses that show how the applicant's experience relates to the volunteer position. Do not write down subjective comments.

If the volunteer assignment requires presentation of documentation, it is sound risk management to obtain the volunteer's permission for the nonprofit to verify these documents. For example, you might require a valid driver's license for your state, a DMV record, proof of insurance, fingerprints or other information required to conduct a background check. Here's a sample of a form you can adapt to meet your needs.

SAMPLE

Permission to Verify Documents

Name of Volunteer Applicant _____

Address _____

City _____ State _____ Zip Code _____

Telephone Number(s): (_____) _____

I give [Name of Nonprofit] permission to verify the credentials that I have presented, such as driver's license, DMV record and/or medical licenses.

Signed _____ Date _____

Reference Checks

References are an invaluable screening tool. You should follow up with references provided by the volunteer applicant just as you would for a paid employee position. Sample questions that could be asked of a person providing a reference for an applicant for a volunteer position are featured on page 40.

Screening Reminders

❑ Always base the screening process on the risks posed by the position. Your analysis of the position description should lead to the selection of

Questions to Ask a Reference for a Volunteer Position

General questions:

❐ In what capacity have you known the applicant and for how long?

❐ Would you rehire the applicant? If no, why not?

❐ How does the candidate handle frustration and criticism while on the job?

❐ Was the candidate punctual?

Questions for applicants who will be working with children, the elderly, the disabled or other vulnerable clients:

❐ When and where have you observed the candidate working with young children/the elderly/persons with disabilities?

❐ What is the candidate's philosophy about discipline?

❐ In your opinion, are there any reasons why placing vulnerable clients in the care of the candidate would expose the clients to undue risk or harm?

Question for applicants for mentoring positions:

❐ Would you be comfortable having the applicant assigned to mentor someone in your family?

---

appropriate screening tools. For example, a volunteer position requiring unsupervised, one-to-one contact with a vulnerable client is a high-risk position. A volunteer position whose duties include answering phones in a busy office may be a low-risk position.

❐ Always use the same screening process for every applicant for a particular position.

❐ Obtain applicants' permission through a statement on the application itself to verify information on the application, and check references and official agency records.

❐ Always determine what findings will make an applicant ineligible for consideration *before* you check official agency records. The criteria should relate directly to the job responsibilities.

If the use of official agency records (through a criminal history background check or credit check) uncovers information that will disqualify an applicant for a position, provide the applicant with an opportunity to "correct the record."

❐ *Make certain that you gather all relevant data before making a judgment.* If any red flags are raised during the screening process, ask the applicant for an explanation or follow up in other ways.

❐ *Be sensitive to cultural differences and your own assumptions.* Remember that you're trying to recruit the best people for key volunteer positions, even if they aren't just like you.

❐ *Consider asking the same question in different ways or use several strategies to confirm key information.* To trace an applicant's employment record you might review the application, request clarification during an interview, and then call former employers. Verifiable information, like a driving record, can give you insights that an interview won't provide. Later on you can line up all the answers and see if the dates and locations match.

❐ *Include others in the process.* One person may pick up signals that the other misses. Consider peer interviews or group sessions. Caveat: Limit the number of eyes that have access to sensitive or private information. Only those staffers with a legitimate need to know should review criminal and financial records.

❐ *Be realistic. Be flexible.* Weigh the thoroughness of the screening technique against the risks inherent in the position and the resources of your nonprofit. For example, a youth-serving organization may want to sponsor a mentoring program that includes overnight visits. If the group doesn't have the resources to screen each volunteer thoroughly, it may revise the program to prohibit unsupervised contact.

❐ *Don't collect information you can't evaluate or that isn't relevant to the position or the selection decision.* Ask yourself what you will do with the information. Some organizations set up elaborate interviewing processes or use personal-style tests such as Myers-Briggs. Yet the person filling the position may not be in position to distinguish an E-N-F-P (extroverted, intuitive, feeling, perceiving) from a J-E-R-K.

❐ *Make sure the information you gather is really necessary and appropriate based on the position description and the nature of the nonprofit.* Do you really need to obtain fingerprints from a prospective volunteer who will be reading to a blind client in the public library?

❐ *Be consistent.* If background checks are important for certain volunteers, they are equally important for all applicants seeking placement in that particular volunteer position. Failing to screen board members, prominent citizens, or others due to their status in the organization or the community invites disaster.

❐ *Don't rely exclusively on a single screening technique.* For example, while criminal records checks may be an important screening tool for certain volunteer positions, other tools are perhaps equally important, such as reference checks.

❐ *Don't make the mistake of believing that a program is too valuable to let thorough screening get in the way.* Although screening procedures may seem daunting, keep your focus on protecting the people you serve and fulfilling your mission.

The next page features sample language granting permission to check information contained on the application, as well as official agency records. Before adopting a new application or making changes to your current application, it's a good idea to consult with legal counsel.

Disclaimer Language
for a Volunteer Application*

Please note that the disclaimer language featured below is not appropriate for all volunteer assignments. Low-risk volunteer positions should probably not be subject to the rigorous review and scrutiny contemplated in this disclaimer. Before using disclaimer language, give some thought to how it will be perceived by prospective volunteers and modify the language to meet the specific needs of your nonprofit.

Read Carefully Before Signing This Application

I hereby consent to permit [Name of Nonprofit] to contact anyone it deems appropriate to investigate or verify any information provided by me to discuss my suitability for a volunteer position, including my background, volunteer experience, education or related matters. I expressly give my consent to any discussions regarding the foregoing and I voluntarily and knowingly waive all rights to bring an action for defamation, invasion of privacy, or similar cause of action, against anyone providing such information.

I hereby authorize any organization affiliated with [Name of Nonprofit] to investigate my background as necessary for the consideration of my application for the position of _____.

I further authorize all persons, schools, companies, organizations, credit bureaus and law enforcement agencies to supply all information concerning my background and to furnish reports thereon. I hereby release them and any organization affiliated with [Name of Nonprofit] from any and all liability and responsibility arising from their doing so.

I certify that the answers given by me to all questions on this application and any attachments are, to the best of my knowledge and belief, true and correct and that I have not knowingly withheld any pertinent facts or circumstances. I understand that any omission or misrepresentation of fact in this application may result in refusal of or separation from volunteer service upon discovery thereof.

Applicant's Signature _____ Date _____

Supervising Volunteers

Securing Volunteer Records

Volunteer records, including applications and the results of reference and background checks, should be treated with the same degree of care that you would afford personnel records. The filing cabinets where volunteer records are kept should be secured at the end of each workday. Access to volunteer files, particularly if these files are stored electronically, should be limited to those with administrative rights and, of course, always should be password protected.

Providing Guidance

Volunteers need to know what they can expect in the way of guidance and supervision. Unclear directions, along with difficulty in contacting a supervisor for guidance, can result in frustration for the volunteer, and can easily lead to making mistakes, or inappropriate behavior. Supervision of volunteers is essential in carrying out the objectives of the program, and in providing services in a consistent manner. Lack of adequate supervision can lead to clients perceiving that they are being treated in a differently—primarily because one volunteer provides assistance in one way, and a second in quite another manner. Food bank clients might believe that they are being discriminated against if volunteer "A" routinely gives them a few "extra" groceries, but volunteer "B" gives the prescribed amount. In reality, volunteer "A" is the culprit and isn't doing either the food bank or the clients any favors. It's important to explain to volunteers why the rules exist, and the implications to the organization and the clients if rules are ignored.

Progressive Discipline and Terminating the Relationship With a Volunteer

It's never easy to have to tell staff members, paid or unpaid, that their performance is unsatisfactory. However, it's very important that volunteers understand that their duties need to be carried out in a manner that is consistent with the organization's mission and operational standards.

Checklist for Volunteer Supervision

☐ Does your nonprofit have a *volunteer handbook* or similar document that contains all of the policies that apply to volunteers?

☐ Do you have a *grievance policy/procedure* or other strategy for receiving and taking action on volunteer complaints?

☐ Are all volunteers required to sign an *acknowledgment* indicating that they have read and agree to abide by the nonprofit's policies?

☐ Are volunteers subject to *discipline*, up to and including removal, for failing to follow the nonprofit's policies?

☐ Are the nonprofit's *disciplinary procedures* concerning volunteers applied consistently?

☐ Are supervisors of volunteers trained in *performance counseling* so they are in position to help a volunteer address performance weaknesses?

When a volunteer's performance needs to be modified, the first step in some organizations may be to counsel the volunteer regarding the steps that must be taken to improve performance. Perhaps the situation can be remedied by providing additional training or pairing the person with a more experienced volunteer. In other instances, the volunteer needs to be counseled regarding behavioral issues.

It's a very sad day when a nonprofit needs to terminate its relationship with a volunteer, but in some cases the organization could find itself in more difficult straits if the volunteer is retained. Generally speaking, the termination should be carried out by the volunteer's supervisor, with a third person present. The reasons for the termination should be explained.

The Nature of the Assignment and the Risk Involved

In a typical nonprofit organization, there are multiple categories of volunteers, some are members of the board of directors, some work in the office, some work with clients and some work on special projects or perform other short-term assignments. Each volunteer category brings with it risk management issues and challenges. In this section, we'll examine the characteristics of each of these categories and the ways in which risk management practices can be incorporated into volunteer administration.

■ **Board Members**

Board members are the people that the organization looks to for leadership and policy making. Typically, these are very busy individuals whose lives can include a full-time paid position or a host of other volunteer commitments. These individuals have fiduciary and other legal obligations associated with their status in the organization. However, the well-being of the organization is contingent upon the competence and commitment that this group brings to the table. When the board is merely a collective figurehead, then the oversight obligations suffer, and the situation can quickly deteriorate into a crisis. The board of a well-known human services agency was lax and apathetic regarding the organization's management until a financial scandal rocked the nonprofit. Their contract with the city for the provision of housing was cancelled, and the organization was reduced to approximately one-third of its original size, and lost more than $1 million in donations. Negative publicity dogged the agency, and it took almost eight years for the organization to restore its credibility in the public eye.

Could effective volunteer administration have prevented this tragedy? Possibly, by strengthening the board's leadership and providing tools for the board to meet its legal duties of care, loyalty and obedience. Information on these legal duties and some measures an organization can take to empower its board are provided on pages 17-19.

Board members, as unpaid volunteer staff, need to understand that their position in the nonprofit organization comes with a set of explicit expectations. These expectations need to be clearly stated in writing in the board of directors binder or packet that is given to each board member—and updated at regular intervals. These expectations also need to be stated in a clear concise manner at the board orientation, as both instruction for the new members and review for the seasoned members.

Interaction with the paid staff can pose problems for board members if expectations aren't made clear from the start. Board members have *one* employee—the executive director of the nonprofit organization. If the board doesn't approve of the performance of a paid staff member, the appropriate procedure is to discuss this disapproval with the executive director. It's never appropriate for a board member to express disapproval directly to the individual staff member. Board members should avoid meddling in the day-to-day operations of the organization. They should not ask, demand or request special favors or consideration from paid staff. However, board members do have an obligation to bring to the attention of the executive director any material information that might affect personnel decisions.

A board member in a nonprofit was advised by a professional associate that the individual recently hired as development director had a reputation for résumé embellishment and was held in some disrepute among other development directors in that city. The board member immediately reported this information to the executive director and requested that the executive director review the hiring procedures in this case. It turned out, the board member's associate was correct. The résumé that the development director had presented contained numerous inaccuracies and the individual's background and references hadn't been thoroughly checked. The executive director confronted both the development director (who was subsequently dismissed) regarding the inaccuracies and the human resources director for failing to do an adequate background check. Confronting the development director was *not* the purview of the board member, but correctly the purview of the executive director.

■ **Volunteers Who Work in the Nonprofit's Programs**

The volunteers who work in a nonprofit's programs represent an invaluable resource to the organization. They work on a daily, weekly or monthly basis. Some have been volunteering with your nonprofit for many years; some may have just started. All programmatic volunteers should have up-to-date records, a fresh orientation, and possibly a skill upgrade or training to expand their skills. They may also need to provide current documentation.

At least annually, the director of volunteers should review these records to ensure that they are current. Request that volunteers provide the organization with current address and contact information and documentation, such as a recent motor vehicle record from the state Department of Motor Vehicles, proof of personal automobile insurance and a current driver's license. If they are working with children, the elderly, disabled clients or other vulnerable populations, additional screening tools may be appropriate. Explain why it's important to include information on who to call in case of emergency, and why it's important to maintain contact information. Review position descriptions to ensure that any and all tasks are relevant and reflect what the volunteer is really doing on the job. The review of records might be a good time to meet with the volunteer to do a "check-in" to see if the volunteer assignment is still satisfactory and meeting the needs of both the volunteer and the organization. Perhaps a change is as good as a rest.

The section on volunteer records on page 44 provides a beginning framework for developing or refining the records system for direct service volunteers.

Curriculum Design for Orientation

An orientation is really a brief course in the nonprofit's history, mission, vision and programs, and where and how the volunteer fits into all of this. The orientation needs to engage, enlighten, motivate and, above all, inform the participants enough to prevent boredom—and get the message across. Here's a basic outline for a volunteer orientation. Clearly each organization needs to customize it, but it provides a basic framework.

SAMPLE

Volunteer Orientation Agenda

Recommended Time	Topic	Action
10 minutes	Welcome	Welcome the volunteers to the organization.
	Introduction	Include paid staff from the nonprofit, particularly those who work directly with volunteers. In an icebreaker exercise, pair the volunteers and paid staff, and have each one interview the other and use the information they learn to introduce the other.
5 minutes	Nonprofit's History and Mission	Understanding the history and mission of the organization is essential to volunteers, particularly as the mission of the organization provides the basis for the nonprofit's programs. If the history of the organization is lengthy, just give the significant highlights. It's particularly important to clearly link the ways in which the organization's mission has been played out over the history of the agency.

continued on next page

Recommended Time	Topic	Action
15 minutes	Volunteering	Describe the history of volunteer involvement in the organization. This discussion needs to clearly link the organization's mission with the history of involving volunteers. Participants need to be able to understand how their volunteer assignments help to accomplish the organization's mission. The overview of opportunities should cover the variety of volunteer assignments within the organization. If possible, paid staff and/or other volunteers should describe these opportunities and the categories of tasks or other commitments, such as time or length of assignment, relevant to the responsibility.
30 minutes	Performance	This segment of the orientation is crucial to articulating expectations of performance and behavior. The discussion needs to be clear and straightforward. It's particularly important to include a discussion about how volunteers will be evaluated. Address issues related to public relations and volunteer service. Make volunteers aware of the implications that staff performance— paid and unpaid—has on the level of confidence clients, stakeholders and members of the public have in the nonprofit. Explain what the volunteer's role is in maintaining the public's trust, and how the way in which clients, stakeholders and the public are treated reflects on the organization. Discuss prohibited behaviors. Describe the organization's policies on drugs/alcohol, sexual harassment and any others that define prohibited behaviors and their consequences. Emphasize that the prohibited behaviors and the consequences apply to *all* staff regardless of their pay status.
		Include what volunteers can expect from the organization. Volunteers need to know that the organization has a grievance process and that issues related to assignments or working conditions should be brought to the attention of the director of volunteers who is willing to work with volunteers to resolve problems.

Recommended Time	Topic	Action
5 minutes	Volunteer Handbook	Distribute the volunteer handbook. Review the categories, tell the participants where to view the handbook on the nonprofit's Web site. Explain that they will receive copies of the revisions as they are published and can read them on the Web also.
15 minutes	Questions & Answers	

There is a sample on page 52 of a form that could be signed by a volunteer to indicate that he or she attended the volunteer orientation, received the volunteer handbook and will abide by the organization's protocols and procedures.

Volunteer Handbook

Providing each volunteer with a personal copy of a complete volunteer handbook is a good risk management strategy. Handbooks should be distributed no later than the volunteer orientation session. It's helpful to present the handbook as a *living document*. Many volunteer programs are choosing to post the handbook on a Web site, to enable easy access to volunteers who spend time online. If the handbook is available online, an organization might consider offering relevant links for information on volunteerism, facts on volunteer work, and opportunities within the organization for supplementary assignments.

Every volunteer program's handbook will differ based on the history, programs and perspective of the organization. Effective handbooks contain brief summaries of essential information and help avoid the possibility that a volunteer will be unaware of critical procedures or rules. A sample table of contents is provided on the next page.

SAMPLE
Volunteer Handbook
Table of Contents

- ❏ Mission and history of the organization

- ❏ Description of essential programs

- ❏ Review of relevant information from the volunteer orientation

- ❏ Overview of the volunteer screening process

- ❏ Expectations of volunteers and/or code of conduct

- ❏ Prohibited behavior/conduct

- ❏ Grievance policy for volunteers

- ❏ Operational guidance [Who to contact if you can't make it to your assignment, who to speak to if you have questions about your position, and how to go about requesting a new assignment.]

SAMPLE
Volunteer Orientation and Handbook
Acknowledgment

Name _____

Address _____

City _____ State ____ Zip Code _____

Telephone Number (_____)_____

Date of orientation _____

I have attended [Name of Nonprofit]'s orientation for volunteers and have received and reviewed the [Name of Nonprofit]'s Volunteer Handbook. I agree to abide by the procedures and protocols outlined in the handbook.

Signed _____Date _____

Volunteer handbooks provide new and experienced volunteers with information that they need to do their jobs well, stay in contact with their supervisors and provide excellent service to the organization's clients.

Special Issues for Volunteer Administration

Orientation

Orientation sessions are crucial for providing scope of service and guidelines for conduct. You may want to assign an experienced volunteer to work alongside each new volunteer so that you can observe and guide the new volunteers in working with your client base. In some cases, it's appropriate to prohibit unsupervised one-to-one contact with a vulnerable client (child, mentally or physically challenged person or frail elderly) until the orientation period is completed.

Complaints

Client complaints should be taken seriously and investigated promptly. Caregivers of the clients should understand that the organization has taken appropriate steps to screen paid and unpaid staff, and that other service protocols have been established to protect clients from harm. Caregivers should be encouraged to contact a specific person within the organization if they have any questions, concerns or complaints.

Day-of Volunteers: Short-Term, Large Numbers

Special events often involve large numbers of volunteers who are either recruited in advance, or are encouraged to come on the day of the event. Of course, early recruitment and training are ideal, but sometimes event planning doesn't permit much lead time. However, it's possible to use some lead-time in planning for assignments, brief orientations and supervision.

If possible, obtain some basic data on "day-of" volunteers prior to the event. People who sign up on your nonprofit's

Web site can provide name, address and telephone numbers, and submit their information to you via e-mail. You could also let them check off the preferred area(s) in which they want to work.

It's important to ensure that all volunteers know who they need to report to, and ensure that your volunteers actually report to that supervisor. Supervisors need to have a list of people they will be working with and how to reach these volunteers. Some organizations using "day-of" volunteers require that all volunteers check in on site, complete an emergency contact card and receive instructions about their assignment for the day. Volunteers may also be directed to a supervisor who will provide a safety briefing. A "table of organization" for the event is another means to track the volunteers. The table shows the volunteers assigned to each task area for a specific time frame—and the name of the supervisor(s) for that task area.

"Day-of" volunteer programs generally preclude the use of basic, moderate and rigorous screening processes. It doesn't make practical sense to check references for someone volunteering to be part of the Re-enactment of the Battle of Bull Run, particularly when 10,000 volunteer re-enactors are expected. Whenever the screening process for volunteers must be curtailed or skipped altogether, an organization should compensate by providing additional supervision. For example, volunteers working with money should work in pairs or groups of three. A staff member or longtime volunteer leader should oversee money-collection activities. Sufficient change should be provided; volunteers should be prohibited from "making change" from their own funds. Responsible personnel should retrieve funds at regular intervals. Under no circumstances should any staff member—paid or unpaid—be permitted to take the funds home.

Working With Large Numbers of Volunteers

In a crisis, sometimes volunteers just walk in off the street wanting to help. A widely publicized catastrophe may draw volunteers from around the country or the far corners of the globe. It may be essential to accept volunteers without much, if any screening, but each volunteer should be asked to provide the name and phone number of a contact person, and show a valid driver's license or photo ID from which the organization can make a photo copy or record the ID number.

Briefing volunteers on the type of work that they'll be doing and what's expected of them is essential. Because there's a large ratio of volunteers to supervisors, it's crucial that all volunteers know who their supervisor is and how to be in immediate contact with this person. The supervisor might carry a pager, walkie-talkie or wireless phone. In turn, volunteers need access to a telephone or walkie-talkie to contact the supervisor. When volunteers need to contact a supervisor, but find that they are unable to do so—or it's a colossal hassle— then they sometimes make decisions which might not be what the organization wanted, or they might provide services that the organization didn't intend. Quality supervision means being available when the volunteer needs help to assure that the right thing is done in the way you want it done.

Only those volunteers who have had an orientation, training and some experience with the organization should be permitted to work with valuable organizational resources such as money, supplies or goods for distribution.

Volunteers Out of Country

Religious organizations are among nonprofits that take volunteers out of the country to fulfill their missions. Some additional precautions include checking with the U.S. State Department for travel restrictions, immunizations, appropriate passports, visas and/or other identification to re-enter the country, signed permission from parents or guardians of underage children, and signed medical release forms.

Conclusion

Volunteers are a bona fide component of a nonprofit's human resources. As such, management of unpaid volunteer staff should have a strong parallel to those protocols and practices found in the management of paid staff. The integration of risk management practices into a volunteer program is crucial to its success and a means by which volunteers are trained and supervised to provide excellent service. While it is important to integrate risk management into every volunteer program, the need to do so may be especially important when a nonprofit engages young volunteers. The topic of engaging young volunteers is addressed in Chapter 5.

Chapter 5
Young Volunteers

The participation of children of all ages in community service has become common place during the past decade. According to *Engaging Youth in Lifelong Service*, a report published by Independent Sector (www.independentsector.org) and Youth Service America (www.ysa.org):

❑ Forty-four percent of adults volunteer and two-thirds of them began volunteering their time when they were young.

❑ High school volunteering recently reached the highest levels in the past 50 years.

❑ In every income and age group, those who volunteered as youth donate money and volunteer more than those who did not.

From the involvement of young people on nonprofit boards (www.youthonboard.org) to promoting community-service as a graduation requirement, nonprofits and young people reap substantial benefits when youth participate in volunteer activities. Many of these benefits are well-known and appreciated by nonprofit leaders, policy-makers, parents and more.

Benefits to Young Volunteers

By serving as volunteers in community-based nonprofits, young people have the opportunity to:

- acquire valuable life skills, such as leadership, that will serve them well as they grow to adulthood.

- improve confidence and self-esteem.

- learn to embrace new challenges and opportunities.

- explore fields for future academic study or employment.

- gain an understanding of their roles and responsibilities as public citizens.

- apply the lessons of an academic experience to real world situations.

Benefits to Nonprofits

By engaging young volunteers nonprofits have the opportunity to:

- positively inspire young people outside the nonprofit's client/service-recipient population.

- teach skills that will later be put to use in employment and volunteer positions.

- inspire a life-long appreciation for community service and volunteerism.

- insure that the organization's leadership reflects the population served by the nonprofit.

School Adds Service as Graduation Requirement

A growing trend is the addition of community-service as a requirement for graduation from public and private schools. An example of a school that has taken this step is Healdsburg High School in Healdsburg, CA. Beginning with the Class of 2004, each student must provide "40 hours of voluntary community involvement" to be eligible for graduation (see www.hhs.husd.com/communityservice.html).

Whether these students or the young people in your nonprofit are truly volunteers or are students trying to fulfill graduation requirements, there are risks associated with deploying young people to perform good works in nonprofits and voluntary organizations. While all of the advice in this book can be applied to programs involving young people, this chapter examines and presents additional measures and strategies that deserve special attention when your volunteer workforce consists of or includes under-age personnel. We begin by examining the legal responsibility a nonprofit assumes when it involves young people and continue with the need for careful supervision of young volunteers, the risks of harm caused by adult participants or staff, and the risks of unacceptable behavior on the part of the young volunteer.

Your Nonprofit's Legal Responsibility to Young People

By including young participants as volunteers, your organization assumes a duty to exercise a *reasonable degree of care* to protect them from *foreseeable harm*. This may mean that you will need to assume a greater duty to protect your young participants than you will to safeguard your adult volunteers. You may, for example, be required to exercise greater supervision for young people than for adults. In addition, you may be required to conduct more intensive screening of those who supervise young people than of those who work with adults.

The extent of your duty will depend upon the decisions of the legislatures and courts in the jurisdiction in which your organization operates. The degree of duty may also depend upon the age of the young people involved, upon the nature of your custodial relationship with the young participants and upon other factors that may differ from state to state.

As a rule, the greater the degree of control you maintain over the activities of young people, the greater your duty to protect them from harm. This duty encompasses your need to provide a safe environment and safe materials. You must also select the correct tasks, conduct proper training, and designate adequate and appropriate adult supervisory personnel.

Legal Status of Minors

In most states, individuals under the age of 18 are believed to lack the capacity to enter into a binding contract. Most courts view agreements entered into by minors as "voidable." In essence, a young person may legally enter into the agreement, but may also legally withdraw from that agreement at any time up until (and sometimes after) he or she reaches the age of majority. The voidable nature of these contracts will bear upon your organization's ability to require your young participants to sign waivers, releases and other such documents. This may also have an impact on the ability of young people to serve in any formal capacity on committees or the board of directors of your organization.

According to Youth on Board, "seven states prohibit young people from serving on boards," and "in fourteen states and the District of Columbia, young people are not allowed to incorporate the nonprofit organization." In Michigan, Minnesota and New York there are laws that authorize the involvement of young people on boards while providing some restrictions. For example, the Minnesota law allows young people to serve on boards if the majority of the members are over 18 years of age (Minn. Stat. Section 317A.205). (For more information, see: *Your Guide to Youth Involvement and the Law,* www.youthonboard.org.)

Student Supervision and Safety

Supervising young volunteers and taking steps to protect their safety are important issues for any nonprofit engaging young volunteers. Consider developing a set of rules and policies that minimize the chance that the harm you envision will materialize. For example, a policy requiring signed permission slips provides evidence that a child has permission to volunteer and reduces the chance that a child whose parent does not want them to volunteer will wind up assigned to a service project. Of course, the permission slip must give parents/ guardians sufficient detail that will allow them to decide whether or not their child can participate safely in your program. Identify the types of harm that could occur to young volunteers and list the practical steps your agency will take to reduce the chance of harm and to make certain your agency is prepared to respond if something goes wrong in spite of its efforts.

Many nonprofits develop a basic set of rules that apply to activities involving young service recipients, young volunteers or both. A sample list of rules follows that you might want to consider as you develop policies that reflect and meet the needs of your agency without compromising its mission.

Protecting Young People From Adult Misbehavior

Every nonprofit that involves young people as volunteers recognizes the risk—perhaps remote in most cases—that a young volunteer could suffer harm caused by an adult. The range of potential harm includes physical, emotional and

SAMPLE

SAMPLE
Program Rules

1. All service sites will have continual adult supervision and guidance for young volunteers.

2. Young volunteers will be instructed as to their responsibilities and the reporting relationships for the project.

3. Young volunteers will not be assigned to projects until the organization has received express written permission from a parent/guardian and a medical form providing health and emergency contact information.

3. No young volunteer may be assigned to any activity or project involving the use of dangerous or potentially dangerous tools and/or equipment. In addition, young volunteers will not be assigned to work in hazardous areas of a project work site.

4. Assignments for young volunteers will be made after an assessment of each volunteer's maturity and ability in order to ensure an appropriate match.

5. In no instance will a young volunteer be permitted or requested to drive an automobile on the nonprofit's behalf. This prohibition includes using young volunteers to transport materials/equipment or people in their own vehicles or vehicles owned by the nonprofit. Driving duties are strictly limited to approved drivers over the age of 24.

6. Young volunteers will not be expected or asked to participate in service programs and activities scheduled late in the evening or at very early hours of the day.

7. Young volunteers serving in health facilities will not be assigned any duties leading to exposure to fluids, excretions, or contaminations known to be harmful, contagious, or injurious.

Permission Slip

As the parent/guardian (circle one) of _____[name of student], I hereby grant permission for my child/ward to participate in Clean the Park Day on June 1, 2007. I understand that this event is being sponsored by the Clean Spaces Foundation and that I am solely responsible for determining whether it is appropriate for my child/ward to participate.

In addition to granting permission for my child/ward to participate, I also authorize the provision of emergency medical treatment in the event of a medial emergency. The number where I can be reached on the day of the event should an emergency arise is _____.

Name of parent/guardian _____

Signature _____ Date _____

sexual abuse. While it is up to your nonprofit to determine how and when harm could happen and what practical measures are called for, the following list offers strategies that other youth involving and youth-serving nonprofits have adopted in order to protect the young people in their programs.

❏ Minimize the risk of harm to young people by providing two-deep leadership for all activities. At least two adults should be present for all programs sponsored by the nonprofit, thereby avoiding isolation of a young person with an adult.

❏ Instruct adult staff and volunteers about inappropriate and appropriate conduct. For example, under what circumstances is it appropriate to offer or give a hug to a young volunteer? What actions/behaviors are strictly prohibited, such as offering a young volunteer a ride home or striking up a personal relationship with a volunteer outside the bounds of the program?

❑ Instruct young volunteers on appropriate and inappropriate conduct with adult staff and volunteers. Explain who they should contact to report misconduct of an adult in the program.

❑ Establish a process for checking in with young volunteers to determine their feelings about the program and determine if there are issues or concerns that require follow-up. The person conducting this follow-up should be someone other that the person(s) directly responsible for supervising volunteers on a day-to-day basis.

Participant Behavior Guidelines

A growing challenge for nonprofits that serve and involve young people is the increase in violence among young people. While behavioral challenges may be more likely in programs serving youth rather than involving youth as volunteers, every nonprofit should consider ways to prevent inappropriate behavior and think through how the organization will respond if this behavior occurs.

The first step in preventing inappropriate behavior is communicating to young volunteers what the program's expectations and requirements are as well as the consequences of failing to adhere to the nonprofit's rules. Many nonprofits have developed codes of conduct that apply to young volunteers or young service recipients. On occasion nonprofit managers wonder whether including items that should be self-evident—such as a prohibition against fighting with other participants—is necessary. Yet experienced program managers report that these rules help the organization communicate the nonprofit's expectations while giving young people advance warning of the consequences of disruptive or otherwise inappropriate conduct. Everyone can't be expected to play by the same rules if they don't know what your rules are.

Consider the value of a code of conduct in your program. Develop a code that takes the unique aspects of your organization into consideration and reflects your ability to enforce and adhere to the code. The samples that follow are provided to help you consider the types of issues that might be suitable for a code in your nonprofit.

SAMPLE

Anytown Recreation Department
Youth Volunteer Code of Conduct

Volunteer Responsibilities:

❑ Volunteers shall be courteous and respectful of adults and fellow volunteers.

❑ Volunteers shall obey rules of the Anytown Recreation Department.

❑ Volunteers shall show respect for the department's property and the personal property of others.

Volunteer Behavior—If a volunteer becomes aware of any potentially dangerous and/or illegal situations regarding weapons, drugs, alcohol, fights, property damage, theft, etc., or has information regarding such, he/she is requested to report it to an Anytown Recreation Department staff member.

Volunteer Behavior Rules—The following is a list of general rules to guide volunteer behavior during Recreation Department activities.

❑ Assault or battery, including sexual assault or battery, upon others is strictly prohibited. In the event an assault or battery occurs, the Department will notify and cooperate fully with local law enforcement in the prosecution of offenders.

❑ Volunteers are expected to follow the instruction of the Recreation Department staff. If a volunteer disobeys any staff member, either by action or word, he/she will be considered defiant. Severe defiance will result in the volunteer's ineligibility to participate in future Department programs.

- Volunteers should consult staff concerning any problems they are having with other volunteers. If a fight occurs, all participants, including bystanders who provoke and encourage such behavior will be subject to suspension. The Department will suspend any volunteer who causes physical injury to another person, unless it results from in self-defense.

- Illegal Substances, Drugs and Alcohol—The use of or possession of any illegal substance during any event sponsored by the Department is grounds for immediate suspension.

- Interpersonal Relationships—Appropriate personal relationships are encouraged. However, holding hands, walking arm-in-arm, hugging and kissing are not appropriate while volunteering.

- Substances—Permanent markers, aerosol spray cans of any type, glue, and correction fluid are not to be brought to any Department activity.

- Swearing, Profanity—Volunteers are not to use profanity or vulgar language. Swearing will not be tolerated. Volunteers will be counseled to be aware of their language. The circumstances will determine if more severe consequences are needed.

- Tobacco, Possession of Tobacco and Smoking—Possession of tobacco or cigarettes, cigarette lighters, or matches, will constitute grounds for suspension. The Department will notify and cooperate with local law enforcement concerning the discovery of the illegal possession of tobacco products.

- Vandalism—Damaging the Department's property or the property of others will not be tolerated. Depending upon circumstances, a police report will be made. Parents or guardians will be liable to pay for damages.

- Weapons, Dangerous—Volunteers are subject to immediate expulsion for possession of any firearm, knife, explosive or other dangerous object while participating in a Department-sponsored program.

I have read and understand the Volunteer Code of Conduct described above. I agree to abide by these rules and acknowledge that violation of any rule could lead to discipline, up to and including immediate expulsion.

Signature _____

Printed Name _____ Date_____

Code of Conduct for Volunteers

The overall experience for volunteers participating in [name of organization or name of event] should promote the development of healthy and positive values towards themselves, fellow volunteers, and adult leaders. The following Code of Conduct has been developed to help increase the positive nature of your experience while volunteering in [name of organization's] programs and activities.

As a participant in our programs, you have a responsibility to:

1. Treat everyone you encounter fairly and with respect, regardless of gender, size, ethnicity, race, sex, age, religion, political beliefs or economic status.

2. Consistently display high personal standards. This requires:

   ❑ Refraining from public criticism of fellow volunteers, adult leaders and employees of [name of organization];

   ❑ Abstaining from the use of tobacco products and encouraging other volunteers to abstain as well;

   ❑ Abstaining from the illegal consumption of alcoholic beverages or possession or use of any legally prohibited substance;

   ❑ Refraining from the use of profane, insulting or otherwise offensive language;

   ❑ Refraining from any conduct that causes damage to or the destruction of the personal property of others; and

   ❑ Treating service recipients, other volunteers and adult supervisors with utmost respect and refraining from any conduct that might be regarded as harassment, disrespectful or otherwise unacceptable to [name of organization].

I have read and understand the above Code of Conduct. I understand that violation of this Code may result in immediate discipline, up to and include dismissal as a volunteer and ineligibility for future involvement.

Name of Volunteer: _____

Signature: _____ Date: _____

Success-Oriented Conduct Codes

Young children, who think in concrete terms, need short, specific rules that they can understand, follow and know when they broke. See sample below:

Rules of Conduct
- ☐ No hitting.
- ☐ No biting.
- ☐ No pinching.
- ☐ No slapping
- ☐ No kicking.
- ☐ No pulling hair.
- ☐ No fighting.
- ☐ No yelling.
- ☐ Report all accidents to your teacher (leader).

School-age children who comprehend abstract concepts, need direction, but can understand broader terms. See sample below.

Rules of Conduct
- ☐ No fighting.
- ☐ No weapons.
- ☐ No drugs, including alcohol, or drug paraphernalia.
- ☐ No swearing or bad mouthing.
- ☐ Report all accidents to a teacher/leader.

The rules should reflect the developmental age of the program's participants.

Conclusion

Young volunteers require training and supervision to keep them safe, concerns that used to cause nonprofits to have second thoughts about accepting help from seniors. Today's seniors have health, energy, motivation and skills to share. How you incorporate their abilities is the focus of Chapter 6.

Chapter 6
Senior Volunteers

S eniors are participating as volunteers for nonprofit organizations in record numbers. From SeniorCorps, the federally-funded national "network of programs that tap the experience, skills, and talents of older citizens to meet community challenges" (source: www.seniorcorps.org) to seniors who serve in large numbers of nonprofits throughout the country, to senior church members, grandparents and others who pursue local volunteer opportunities in human services, recreation, cultural arts and social services.

According to the report *65+ in the United States: 2005*, "1 out of every 5 Americans—some 72 million people—will be 65 years of age or older in 2020. This is 20 percent of the population. The age group 85 and older is now the fastest growing segment of the U.S. population" (source: www.census.gov).

According to a report by Independent Sector and AARP, 47 percent of working Americans 50 years and older volunteer, while 42 percent of retired Americans in this age group volunteer. The report notes, "Retired volunteers aged 50 and over are even more dedicated that those still working...they give substantially more hours per month." (Source: *Experience at Work: Volunteering and Giving Among Americans 50 and Over*, www.independentsector.org). With increases of 31 percent (50-64 years old) and 12.5 percent (65 and older) projected by 2010, older Americans represent a tremendous opportunity for nonprofit and volunteer organizations.

> "Today people over 50 years of age constitute the largest, best-educated, and healthiest group of older Americans in our nation's history. Their numbers will continue to grow as the Baby Boom generation ages and life expectancy lengthens. Older Americans have the richness of diversity reflected in other age demographics. No matter their gender, ethnicity, income level or religion, the one thing they do have in common is a lifetime of experience that makes them a valuable pool of potential volunteers for any organization. As vital, contributing members of society, their skills and experiences can benefit many in their communities."
>
> *Experience at Work: Volunteering and Giving Among Americans 50 and Over*, www.independentsector.org.

The benefits to seniors who volunteer include:

❑ providing an outlet for professional skills, talents and interests.

❑ providing a sense of accomplishment and fulfillment.

❑ providing growth and learning opportunities, keys to a successful aging experience.

The benefits a nonprofit realizes by recruiting senior volunteers include:

❑ access to multitalented, experienced volunteers whose myriad talents can quickly fill a nonprofit's volunteer wish list.

❑ enhancing the volunteer experience for volunteers of all ages by bringing a diverse group of individuals together to work on behalf of a community or cause.

Risk Management Do's and Don'ts When Engaging Seniors in Service

Do:

❑ *Think about the types of assignments and responsibilities senior volunteers will have* in your agency before you begin a targeted recruitment effort. Respect these valuable volunteers by planning for their involvement in your nonprofit well before they arrive at your new volunteer information session or recruitment drive.

❑ *Ask prospective senior volunteers for input* about their involvement in your nonprofit. Find out what tasks they are comfortable performing and what tasks or activities they cannot or do not want to perform.

❑ *Require that senior volunteers, along with other volunteers, complete a Medical Information Form* containing information on special medical conditions (such as allergies), all medications and at what dosage they are taken, and key contact information in the event of a medical or other emergency.

❑ *Engage seniors who let you know about a specific physical or other limitation.* Explore with the seniors what they are comfortable doing or how the task or assignment can be modified to address the limitation rather than rule out the possibility of their participating in the activity or contributing to your agency.

❑ *Learn about the special talents and skills of senior volunteers.* Your fundraising chair or Foster Grandparent may be a retired or working risk manager, and able and willing to serve on your risk management committee in addition to performing program-related service. Or your volunteer senior companion or Meals-on-Wheels driver may be a former salsa instructor who is willing to donate dance lessons to your silent auction.

❑ *Provide a position description for each senior volunteer* in order to convey your expectations with respect to the volunteer's role and responsibilities in your agency. The job description should provide the kind of information the senior volunteer will need to determine whether he or she can fully perform the tasks you require.

- *Include specific job requirements* (e.g., lifting boxes weighing up to 30 pounds) on your volunteer position descriptions. Spelling out specific tasks lets prospective volunteers know what you require while reducing the chance that a mismatch will be made.

- *Schedule regular breaks for volunteers working shifts of two hours or longer.* Encourage all volunteers to let you know when they need to take more frequent rest, stretch or comfort breaks than are scheduled.

- *Provide an orientation and appropriate training for senior volunteers.* Every volunteer needs information about what you expect, as well as resources available to help them succeed while working for you—just as your staff members do in order to perform as you wish.

Finding the Right Role: One Volunteer's Experience

At age 62, Helen approached the prospect of volunteering in a food pantry with excitement and nervous anticipation. The panty's mission of distributing donated food to soup kitchens was appealing, but it had been more than 10 years since Helen last volunteered at her daughter's high school. The other volunteers on her shift at the food pantry seemed nice enough, but the acoustics at the warehouse made it next to impossible to carry on a conversation with her fellow volunteers. And the job required Helen to move and unpack heavy crates containing canned goods donated by local grocery stores. After the first back-breaking day at the pantry, she realized that her history of chronic back pain made it impossible for her to volunteer without jeopardizing her health. The following week, she accepted a volunteer position at a VA Hospital, where her duties include delivering magazines and other items to residents. In this new role Helen is able to interact with residents and staff members while performing a service that is clearly appreciated by consumers and caregivers alike. If you ask Helen, she'll tell you that finding a position that suits your interests, personality and physical capabilities is the key to a rewarding volunteer experience. Could the food pantry have found another role for Helen? If so, they'd still have her as a volunteer.

❑ *Create a welcoming environment* for senior volunteers. If there is a substantial learning curve for service, consider pairing new volunteers with experienced "mentor" volunteers who can show them the ropes. Consider pairing people by age group so as to avoid any resentment an experienced senior might feel being shown how to chop vegetables in a soup kitchen, paint a kitchen wall in a home rebuilding project, or stuff envelopes at an advocacy group by a teenager or young adult. Or educate all your volunteers how to work with people of all ages as part of their volunteer experience.

❑ Strive to *provide flexibility* in work hours and assignments. Keep in mind that all seniors have busy lives that may involve providing child care, caring for elderly parents, managing family matters, other volunteer commitments and more.

❑ *Remember that patience is a virtue* when supervising all volunteers. A senior whose memory "isn't what it used to be" may be among your most active and valued volunteers. The occasional need to repeat instructions is well-worth the benefit you'll reap from dedicated, mature volunteers who believe in your mission. And perhaps it was the instructions that needed fine-tuning and not the senior's hearing or comprehension.

❑ *Encourage senior volunteers to ask questions* while serving your agency. Like volunteers in other age groups, some seniors may be reluctant to ask questions because they fear that the question suggests ignorance or inattentiveness. Gently encourage questions and make certain all your volunteers know "there is no such thing as a dumb question."

Don't:

❑ *Make assumptions about physical or other challenges* facing seniors simply because of their age. Assuming that any volunteer 60 or older will not have the energy for coaching duties, or jobs that require prolonged standing or walking, is a grave mistake.

❑ *Assign senior volunteers "busy work."* Remember that perhaps more so than other groups of volunteers, seniors infrequently look for "one-day" or temporary volunteer opportunities. Don't miss the opportunity to engage a volunteer who will make a meaningful contribution to your nonprofit.

❑ *Exempt senior volunteers from your screening process* because you believe it is disrespectful to screen mature adults or you believe that older people do not pose a risk to vulnerable clients. All prospective workers should be subject to a screening process based on an analysis of the risks of the position. A rigorous process should be employed whenever a volunteer (or paid staff member) will have unsupervised contact with vulnerable clients, whether they are young, disabled or elderly.

Understanding and Managing the Risks

As is true with other groups of volunteers, there are risks that arise when older volunteers work in nonprofit organizations. Some of these risks—such as the risk that a volunteer will have an unsatisfying experience—are common to all volunteer programs. Other risks arise because of the expectations and physical and mental challenges of senior volunteers.

It is possible to safely engage seniors in all forms of service, from new home construction, to coaching, one-to-one mentoring and meal-delivery programs. The possibilities are endless. And given the demographic shifts and the fact that seniors represent a larger than ever percentage of the population, a nonprofit that ignores this group of prospective volunteers misses a mission-fulfilling opportunity.

In the report mentioned at the outset of this chapter, the publishers—Independent Sector and AARP—mention two areas that sometimes pose barriers to volunteer service: disabilities or health concerns, and transportation. Other areas of concern that may arise include program location, community-based service delivery, and judging applicants by age.

In the pages that follow we discuss some of the risks that may arise in deploying senior volunteers and practical strategies for addressing these risks.

Risks Associated With Physical Challenges

While it is not appropriate to assume that senior volunteers face physical challenges, it is important to understand that when these challenges exist, it is still possible to engage volunteers safely in service opportunities. Senior volunteers may face such challenges as visual impairment; hearing loss; dexterity, strength and range of motion; and difficulty walking. As seniors age, the percentage of individuals in a particular age group that have either a disability or chronic health concern increases as well. In some cases, a nonprofit will not be sufficiently equipped to fully involve seniors with disabilities or chronic health concerns. However, in many cases minor modifications can be made—at minimal cost—to allow barrier-free access to and use of a volunteer program's offices and program space.

Inexpensive fixes that can be made to make your work space senior-friendly include:

❑ Replacing toggle light switches with rocker-style switches that are easy to operate by all.

❑ Installing spacer rings and thick seats that raise the height of existing toilets, or replace toilets with new models with seats 19 inches above the floor.

❑ Replacing existing cabinet and drawer pulls with U-shaped (C or D ring) pulls and handles, which are easier to grip and pull, and make the contents accessible to all of your volunteers.

- ❑ Installing simple threshold ramps in areas where a threshold creates an unnecessary tripping hazard.

- ❑ Removing or taping down any loose carpets or tiles.

- ❑ Replacing doorknobs and thumb latches with door levers that are easy to manipulate by all.

Risks Associated With Transportation and Driving

Another concern raised by Independent Sector and AARP is that some seniors may face difficulty getting to volunteer programs that do not offer ample, free parking (with parking spaces close to the entrance) or close access to public transportation. While a mile hike to the subway or bus might be an acceptable commute for a teenage or young adult volunteer, a senior volunteer might be dissuaded from serving if getting to your service site is too exhausting.

Driving at night might be a problem because of reduced nightvision or reduced peripheral vision. Public transportation may not be an option in the evening if your agency is located in an area perceived as less safe. Yet, evening might be the time when older employed volunteers are available to donate time and skills.

One option for addressing both these concerns is to consider ways to involve senior volunteers working from home, or working in groups at a convenient location. For example, a volunteer program might connect with a church, local quilting group, historic preservation society or other group that has a defined meeting place and arrange to provide volunteer opportunities at this existing, convenient location. Another option is to arrange carpool service for senior volunteers.

Driving-Related Concerns

If the volunteer position requires driving, you'll want to be certain that the driver has a current permit for your state, that there are no restrictions (such as no night driving) that would disqualify them for the assignment, and that they have appropriate insurance, if they will be driving their own car for your nonprofit. If they are driving the organization's vehicle, the same checkpoints apply, except that you want to make certain your commercial automobile insurance is adequate and current. Some older drivers are more comfortable driving a set route; others like to strike out for parts unknown. Ask questions and match the appropriate skill and comfort level to the task at hand.

Risks Associated With Location

Your location could be a deterrent to older volunteers who may perceive that your location places them at greater risk than their home or work locale. Whether this fear is backed up by crime statistics or not, you may have to alter the way you do business in order to gain the participation of these volunteers. You might provide an escort from your parking facility to the building. You could provide a bulletin board where volunteers needing a ride or offering a ride could pair up.

Risks Associated With Service to the Community

Because older volunteers have a different view of mortality than teenage volunteers, they might be wary of going into the community to provide service to your clients. However, your organization may want their experience, ability to relate to your service recipients, and their level of judgment to deliver meals, interview clients or check on the ongoing care of an adopted animal. One statewide group equips each volunteer with a mobile phone for their own protection and peace of mind. Another organization with fewer resources provides personal safety courses to help volunteers and employees be alert and aware of their surroundings. Police officers from the local precinct donate their time and expertise. Another solution might be sending out volunteers in pairs.

Risks Associated With Judging the Applicant by Age

Older volunteers bring a wealth of knowledge and experience. Remember that each person must be judged on his or her own; not as a member of a certain age group. *Don't assume* that the 50-year-old will be more mentally and physically active than the 80-year-old. Use your eyes and ears during the application and interview processes. Watch the person walk; listen for comprehension skills; note facial expression and enthusiasm; ask about interests; and then make the match. If your organization needs people who are physically fit and a sister organization has lots of volunteer slots for sedentary work, set up a referral system. Your organization will be remembered as gracious and helpful, the sister organization will gain a willing participant and the entire nonprofit sector will reap the benefits.

Conclusion

As you rethink access issues, supervision, communication and skills to welcome volunteers of 50 plus years, make adaptations that will benefit all volunteers. RespectAbility, www.respectability.org, helps each nonprofit involve older Americans more effectively in the organization's mission. Chapter 7 addresses the growing field of pets as volunteers. Many nonprofits involve animals in providing services to their clients.

Chapter 7
Pets as Volunteers

P ets are taking a more active role in the volunteer scene. They can become working guide dogs, companions and healers. But just as you want make certain the people volunteering with vulnerable clients are of the right temperament and will do no harm, you want to make certain the animals are appropriate, too.

Animals also can assist their owners; as ears for those who can't hear, eyes for those who can't see and arms and legs for those who have little use of their own. People volunteer with their pets through animal-assisted activities and animal-assisted therapy.

According to Delta Society (www.deltasociety.org), animal-assisted activities can be casual meet-and-greet events that involve pets and people. In contrast, animal-assisted therapy is a significant part of treatment for many people who are physically, socially, emotionally or cognitively challenged.

Animal-Assisted Activities

Animal-assisted activities provide social, motivational, educational, and/or recreational benefits for people during interactions. Interaction with specially trained animals helps to change lives of discouragement, fear and sadness into one of happiness, independence and hope. These activities don't need to be overseen by healthcare professionals and don't work toward particular clinical goals.

Examples of AAA are:

- ❏ Volunteers take their dogs and cats to nursing home once a month to "visit." The visit is part of a large group activity with some direction and help provided by the home's staff.

- ❏ A person brings her dog to a children's long-term care facility to "play" with residents. The staff is involved but has not set treatment goals for the interactions. Except for signing in and out, no records are kept of the visit.

- ❏ A dog obedience club gives an obedience demonstration at a residential facility for teens with delinquent behavior.

Delta Society's *Pet Partners* program trains volunteers and screens their pets for participation in animal programs in hospitals, nursing homes, rehabilitation centers and schools. Delta Society-licensed instructors train volunteers and their pets through hands-on workshops or a home study course and a continuing education newsletter. Before the animals visit the facilities, they are tested for skills and aptitude by the society's licensed animal evaluators.

The society has a national network that links volunteers and facilities in their own communities and helps Pet Partners contact facilities to begin visits in new locations. There are more than 8,000 teams of Pet Partners in the United States and four other countries that provide more that 900,000 hours of community service annually. Registered pets include dogs and cats, as you would expect, but also guinea pigs, rabbits, horses, goats, llamas, donkeys, potbellied pigs, cockatoos, African grey parrots and chickens.

Animal-Assisted Therapy

Animal-assisted therapy is a goal-directed intervention. It is sometimes called pet-facilitated therapy and animal-facilitated therapy. The animal is an integral part of the treatment plan.

AAT is directed and/or delivered by a health or human service professional with a particular clinical goal in mind. A therapist who uses AAT want to create a change in the person through the client's or patient's interaction with the animal. Physical therapists, occupational therapists, certified therapeutic recreation specialists, recreational therapists, teacher, social workers and other can weave AAT into their work.

The therapy animal is usually the personal pet of its handler, who remains in the room during the session. The animal works in animal-assisted activities and animal-assisted therapy. Visiting animal-handler teams (such as those trained through Pet Partners) are the most common source of therapy animals. The handlers of the visiting teams may be volunteers or healthcare professionals. Service animals and residential animals can also be integrated as therapy animals.

Healthcare professional who want to use their own animals for AAT can register as Delta Society Pet Partners or through other registries. Registration helps give legitimacy to the AAT program.

Policies, procedures and administrative issues should be determined prior to the implementation of an AAT program. And healthcare professionals should become familiar with key elements of AAT, such as treatment methods, animal behavior and welfare, and current research.

Examples of AAT:

❑ Volunteer and her cat work with an occupational therapist at a rehabilitation center. As part of improving a child's fine motor skills, the child opens containers of treats and feeds small pieces to the cat.

❑ As part of an AAT session to improve a client's ability to sequence events, a therapist teaches a client the steps of brushing a dog. Brushing the dog helps the client remember the steps.

❑ To motivate a recovering stroke patient to increase her tolerance of standing and walking, the therapist has her stand to pet a visiting dog and take the dog for a short walk.

Service Animals

The Americans with Disabilities Act (Federal Code of Regulations, 1990) defines service animals as individually trained to do work or perform tasks for the benefit of a person with a disability (a physical or mental impairment that substantially limits one or more of the major life activities of the individuals). Federal law permits qualified people, who have disabilities, to be accompanied by their service animals in all places of public accommodation, including places with posted "no pet" policies. Service animals are not considered "pets." NOTE: Therapy animals do not benefit from this provision.

Animals can be trained to open doors, answer telephones, load and unload groceries from the cart to the car to the kitchen counter, turn lights on and off, do laundry and even warn people with epilepsy of impending seizures so that the person can get to a safe place before the seizure starts.

Insurance

Registered Pet Partners are covered by liability insurance when volunteering, but Pet Partners that professionals using AAT during staff time aren't covered by the Delta Society insurance program. Thus, nonprofits that wish to incorporate pets and owners into client service, might want to look for certified Pet Partners. You can learn more about the program on Delta Society's Web site: www.deltasociety.org/ VolunteerAboutInsurance.htm.

Conclusion

When involving pets and other animals as part of your nonprofit's volunteer program, be as careful screening, training and supervising the animal as you are with the owner/handler. The Delta Society and other registries can help you in your selection process.

Chapter 8
Corporate Volunteers Require Extra Care

A corporate volunteer program is set up by a business to encourage its employees to serve as volunteers within the local community. Corporations may refer to volunteer service as *pro bono* work, board membership, corporate social responsibility, civic involvement, in-kind services or community service. Some companies have a formally structured program administered by employees, while others contract with a nonprofit organization such as a Volunteer Center to run the program. Corporations may choose to sponsor a volunteer program—just as some individuals choose to make charitable donations—for business reasons. However, demonstrating humanitarian concern and social responsibility may be beneficial to a business on a number of fronts. Many business leaders have a sincere desire to give something back to the communities, organizations and people that have made them successful.

In its 1999 report, *The Corporate Volunteer Program as a Strategic Resource: The Link Grows Stronger*, the Points of Light Foundation notes that many corporations link their corporate volunteer programs to their strategic business goals. The report states that, in 1992, only 31 percent of companies said they used their corporate volunteer programs to "support core business functions." By 1999 this number had grown to more than 80 percent.

Clearly more companies are considering CVPs as part of the corporate persona. Today, being a good corporate citizen means more than just offering fair wages and paying business taxes on time.

Regardless of the motives, a CVP isn't risk free. The significant accomplishments of a program can be completely undone if a client or volunteer suffers serious harm while participating in the program. Corporate volunteer programs can place employees and managers in situations beyond their expertise and training or out of their comfort zone. An employee who works in the graphic design unit at a large company may be totally unequipped to mentor young children or volunteer in a soup kitchen or homeless shelter. The employee might even have some factor in his or her background of which management is unaware that makes some community service opportunities inappropriate.

The following are strategies for improving the safety of a corporate volunteer program.

❏ **Establish Your Purpose and Goals**—The first step in safeguarding a program is to determine why the parties (the business or group of businesses and the nonprofit sponsor) want to establish a corporate volunteer program in the first place. Too often, someone has a great idea and everyone jumps on the bandwagon without thinking through the details. One factor to consider is how a corporate volunteer program fits into the business' corporate mission and culture. The chance for success is less if the program doesn't help the corporation and the nonprofit partner fulfill their respective goals. Therefore, it's important to examine why both organizations want to have a corporate volunteer program. At this step it's also wise to look at the various program models and determine which model works best.

Examples of various types of corporate volunteer programs include:

1. Informal Program

2. Matchmaker Program,

3. Sponsorship, and

4. In-house Program.

In an informal program, the company takes a very passive role in offering employees the opportunity to volunteer. The activity can be as small as allowing employees to solicit other employees for donations, pledges and volunteer activities. For example, the firm may permit employees to solicit their co-workers for pledges for a walk-a-thon, sell candy as a fundraiser, or to recruit people to help with a special event. In a matchmaker program, the business is more involved in the employees' volunteer activities by facilitating the matchup of employees to volunteer opportunities. In a sponsorship program, the corporation "sponsors" an activity of the nonprofit organization. The sponsorship can include providing support through the giving of cash, goods and services that identify the company with the activity. The company can provide transportation to and from the event for its employees or sponsor overall transportation services for the event. Often a company will encourage its employees to help with the event either as volunteers or as participants, such as walking or bicycle riding in a fundraiser.

Another example is when the company sponsors certain volunteer activities. The company may coordinate and staff a field trip for the clients of a nonprofit, such as taking children to a zoo or museum, or setting up a lunch-making session at its office for a homeless shelter. Some corporations allow (and some require) their employees to take time off for their volunteer activities. A company with an in-house corporate volunteer program establishes and operates its volunteer program separately from any nonprofit organization. A corporation may choose to set up its own tutoring program for children within the community or other volunteer-based program. Many corporations have internal mentoring programs where a more senior employee mentors a less experienced employee.

The business partner should identify the goals and objectives for the program. How many employee-volunteers will be involved? How many volunteer hours will be committed? With how many and which types of nonprofit organizations or governmental entities will the business form a relationship? Are there any geographic limitations to the program? Does the business want to involve the employees' families and friends in the volunteer efforts? These are just some of the possible questions to ask when establishing or evaluating a corporate volunteer program.

❑ **Plan Carefully**—Develop a timetable for the various activities, including who is responsible for each step of the process. Establish the methods for monitoring the success of the program, including proper record keeping and documentation.

A part of the planning and risk management process is to identify your risks and select the appropriate risk management techniques. Don't forget to develop the policies and procedures needed for your corporate volunteer program. The employees and nonprofit partners need to know the rules and limitations of the program, as well as who to call if there is a problem.

❑ **Know Your Partners**—It's vital that parties on both sides of the equation enter into any collaboration with eyes wide open. Due diligence is critical in increasing the odds of a successful collaboration. Each partner should consider establishing criteria for selecting business or nonprofit organizations with which to work. A corporation might choose organizations based on their tax-exempt status or geographic areas of operation. For example, Oracle among many others will only work with organizations that are tax-exempt under Section 501 (c)(3) of the Internal Revenue Code (IRC). Some corporations select nonprofits based on the nature of the services they provide. A nonprofit may prefer corporate partners that are based in the community where the nonprofit delivers services.

In addition to the care with which they make the initial selection of their nonprofit partners, some businesses conduct periodic reviews of existing partners. Some employees may have had poor experiences with certain organizations. Nonprofits and businesses are dynamic organizations, and over time suitable partners may become unsuitable.

❑ **Get Commitments in Writing**—Most companies put their business deals with other entities in writing to minimize the possibility of a dispute. When a corporation hires a new employee, it uses a job description to make sure that both parties have common understanding about work expectations A lease agreement or contract documents other business dealings. Be as thorough in solidifying the details of a corporate volunteer program as you are in other business dealings.

Commitments and agreements between the corporate volunteer program coordinator and a nonprofit partner should be memorialized in a written document, such as a simple memorandum of understanding. The MOU should outline each party's responsibilities and expectations. Some items to consider are who will be responsible for selecting and screening the volunteers, which party will train and supervise the employee-volunteers and how incidents will be reported and shared with each other. An agreement can have a hold harmless or other indemnification agreement, as well as impose certain insurance requirements on the nonprofit partner. As with any written agreement, memorialize any changes in a document that is signed by both parties.

❑ **Establish Program Policies and Guidelines**— Program policies and guidelines are an extension of the "get it in writing" tip. Every program or activity has its guidelines or procedures, even if they aren't written down. Some of the possible topics the business may want to address in its guidelines include:

➢ whether or not use of corporate facilities is permitted;

➢ whether or not employees serving as volunteers can use company property in their volunteer service, such as vehicles, audio visual equipment, computers, photocopy or facsimile machines, telephones and any other corporate assets that may help them in their volunteering activities;

➤ whether or not the company releases employees from their normal workday to volunteer and whether or not they are paid while volunteering;

➤ whether or not certain activities are considered inappropriate under the program;

➤ whether or not a code of conduct applies to employees participating in the program;

➤ what the selection criteria are for the program;

➤ how employees should document the time they have given to the various nonprofit organizations;

➤ what steps an employee should take in the event of an accident; and

➤ how an employee should report an accident or incident arising from the volunteer program to the company.

❏ **Keep the Lines of Communication Open**—A feedback mechanism is necessary to determine how well the corporate volunteer program is doing. The feedback loop should include employee participants, management at the company and the nonprofit, and service recipients. Establish ways for these different constituencies to share information (good and bad) with the program coordinators. For example, if an employee is involved in an accident (no matter how small) during her volunteer activities, what is she supposed to do? One critical measure of success is the satisfaction of the employee-participants. If volunteering is an unpleasant experience, the participant won't only discontinue her participation but may tell a lot of people about her dissatisfaction. Every employee-participant should know whom to contact either at the company or the nonprofit to discuss any problems or offer suggestions for improving the program.

❑ **Maintain Good Records**—Proper record keeping provides the information needed to evaluate the corporate volunteer program. The extent of the documentation will vary with the structure of the program.

❑ **Consider Insurance: Yours and Theirs**—An important component of a risk management plan for a corporate volunteer program is how it fits into the partner organizations' existing risk financing strategy. It's essential to determine which organization's coverage will apply if someone is injured or property is damaged in the course of delivering the program. In some cases, a corporate partner may impose certain insurance requirements on a nonprofit. As with any collaborative arrangement, reciprocal insurance requirements make good business and risk management sense.

❑ **Evaluate the Results**—Both partners should evaluate the corporate volunteer program to ensure that it's meeting its goals and objectives. Your evaluation system might include statistics on the number of employees involved, the number of hours donated and the number of nonprofit clients served. You can survey employee-participants about their level of satisfaction with the program. Both the nonprofit organization and the business partner should evaluate the quality of the relationship. Any partnership can have its problems but with an effective evaluation system, hopefully, you can identify and resolve any problems quickly.

Conclusion

The relationship with a corporate partner should be scrutinized carefully before entering into a contract. Make certain that all parties are in agreement about responsibilities, insurance, evaluation, and supervision. Have a bail out clause in the agreement that allows parties to dissolve the arrangement amicably. Your foresight will do wonders to maintain positive public relations, the topic of Chapter 9.

Chapter 9
Public Relations Issues in Volunteer Programs

Joan was a new volunteer for the West County Thrift Shop. She was excited about this volunteer opportunity because she felt that her background in retailing could be beneficial in sprucing up the threadbare and rather seedy, old store. Her first day was an eye-opener. That morning a mini-van pulled up and dropped off a treasure-trove of barely worn ladies' clothing including costume jewelry and handbags that looked like they had never been used. The volunteers on duty swarmed the "find" like ants to a pot of honey. Nothing was left for display or the sales racks when they had removed their selections. The volunteers had all declared their "first option" on the merchandise, leaving nothing for the clients of the store. Apparently, having "first option" was a long-standing perk for the volunteers, and the thrift shop management did nothing to stop the practice. Joan was appalled. What Joan observed and experienced was contrary to the mission of the organization. The discovery of this practice could seriously threaten the goodwill of the charity and its reputation in the community.

What's Goodwill and Who Cares?

Goodwill is the trust and confidence your volunteer program has inspired among residents and constituents of your community. The organization's funders support the organization because they believe in what you do, and believe you do what you say you do. These funders include individual donors, grant-making institutions, businesses, and perhaps organizations that purchase services from your organization under contract. None of these people or organizations would support your nonprofit if they thought it was corrupt or poorly run.

Goodwill may be a nonprofit's most valuable and most vulnerable asset. A loss of confidence in a nonprofit can have serious repercussions, ranging from the loss of clients and donors to the departure of valuable staff and volunteers. Some of the ways in which goodwill could be damaged include:

- actions on the part of the board that suggest personal inurement (the transfer of nonprofit assets to an individual), or mismanagement;

- volunteers or paid staff causing harm to clients, such as abuse, molestation, or injuries from alleged carelessness; or

- inappropriate volunteer behavior, including vulgar language or behavior, theft or conversion of property, or inappropriate use of the nonprofit's property.

Any of these or a host of other potentially damaging scenarios could easily harm your organization's reputation and goodwill. The good news is that with the implementation of some sound risk management practices, the potential for this damaging behavior can be reduced.

Volunteer Behavior and Maintaining Public Trust

The public will often judge an organization by the behavior of its paid and unpaid staff. Actually, that's probably the only thing that the public has to go on because the behaviors exhibited by the paid and unpaid staff demonstrate, in the eyes of the observers, the values, culture and vision of the organization. How those individuals with visible affiliation to the organization treat clients and the public speaks volumes. When the behavior and images aren't positive, then the overall reputation of the organization suffers. Even something as superficial as grooming is significant. Volunteers who wear identifying clothing, such as a uniform, should be briefed on the appropriate way in which the uniform must be worn, including such basic but important points as cleanliness, pressing, jewelry and grooming. Volunteers need to know that how they present themselves reflects on the organization and ultimately on how the clients, donors and public view the organization.

Actions Speak Louder Than Words

Behavior and public deportment are particularly important in either reinforcing or contradicting the image of the organization. All people representing the organization, regardless of pay status, have an obligation to conduct themselves in a manner that brings credit to the organization. Often to get volunteers to comply is simply a matter of consciousness-raising. Explaining and providing examples of how behavior, language and actions affect public perception is often sufficient. Include pointers on conflict resolution or customer service to bring home the point.

In more difficult cases, consider what the retail and hospitality industries use—a "secret shopper." The secret shopper is an individual not known to anyone in the organization who poses as a "customer" for the purpose of describing the experience that he/she has had in dealing with the retailer. The management calls the staff together to discuss the secret shopper's findings. The identity of the secret shopper is never disclosed, because the fundamental issue is the quality of service that was provided. The findings are presented in general terms, emphasizing recommendations for improvement in the various components of customer service. The message will be unmistakable that management is serious about evaluating and improving the current level of service.

Loss of Goodwill: What Does That Mean to the Organization?

So what if volunteers dress badly, behave badly, or treat the clients, staff, board or donors in a less than ideal way? With the exception of a major scandal, loss of public trust sometimes happens in small increments, but the cumulative effect can be devastating. Joan might not have been the first volunteer to be shocked at the behavior of the other volunteers at the West County Thrift Shop. Others may have observed the same behavior and either chose to volunteer elsewhere, or described what they observed to others outside the organization.

The loss of goodwill could result in:

❑ loss of competitive positioning for grants or government contracts,

❑ inability to attract new donors or board members,

❑ inability to attract talented paid and volunteer staff,

❑ negative publicity,

❑ inability to find organizations willing to collaborate, and

❑ inability to attract corporate funding.

Loss of Competitive Positioning for Grants or Government Contracts

Contracts with federal, state or local governments may present one option for funding the cost of delivering charitable services. The RFP (request for proposal) process can be arduous and also politically charged. Competition may be fierce among various social services, faith-based organizations and other nonprofits in a particular community. Intangibles such as the organization's reputation and track record in serving clients may have a bearing on whether the organization is able to compete successfully for government contracts.

Inability to Attract New Donors or Board Members

Donors want to believe that they are contributing to a going concern, but also to an organization that will be in operation and serving the community for many years. Donors also want to feel proud of their affiliation with an organization and its staff and volunteers. In particular, individuals who can contribute at the major donor level are often besieged with requests for their money.

Potential board members want to be associated with an organization that is credible, will reflect positively on their personal/professional reputation, and is consistent with their personal values. Nonprofits whose reputations are tarnished have a more difficult time attracting board talent and major donors because these individuals are reluctant to risk their personal/professional reputations and their money on a losing proposition. Current board members may also consider leaving if the reputation of the organization begins to deteriorate. Losing confidence in the nonprofit's management is one of the chief reasons why board members decide to leave prior to the end of their term.

Inability to Attract Talented Paid and Volunteer Staff

Board members and donors aren't the only groups of individuals who would be hesitant to become associated with a nonprofit with a questionable reputation. Talented staff—paid and unpaid—aren't willing to sacrifice their professional and/ or personal reputations. Additionally, marginal nonprofits don't offer much of a future or a place in which to refine one's skills. Ironically, a nonprofit on the skids needs human talent more than ever to bring it back up to a productive level.

Negative Publicity

Whoever said, "There is no such thing as bad publicity," never had to lead a fund-raising campaign in the wake of a scandal, or other adverse news about a nonprofit. At the heart of every fund-raising effort is "selling" prospective donors on supporting or sustaining an organization that has proven itself worthy of such support.

If the source of the negative publicity is the behavior of a board member or other volunteer, the challenge of recouping the organization's good name is even more difficult. Although inappropriate behavior is unpalatable regardless of the pay status of the perpetrator, having a volunteer involved may make the situation worse.

Inability to Collaborate With Other Volunteer Organizations

In the wake of negative publicity, other nonprofits may be unwilling to collaborate with your organization. The inability to partner with other nonprofit organizations spells missed opportunities in a number of areas including special projects featuring the collaboration of like-focused organizations, applying for funding—grants or otherwise—based on cooperative ventures, and the potential to leverage a synergistic relationship to garner more resources. The organization's role in larger forums, such as nonprofit executive director groups or directors of volunteers in agencies, particularly those involving a number of community-based organizations, could be jeopardized.

Inability to Attract Corporate Funding

Negative publicity or problems in the organization's public relations could also cost the nonprofit the opportunity to partner with corporations on various activities. Just as nonprofits should be cautious about selecting appropriate corporate partners, corporations must be cautious about associating with nonprofits that have breached the public trust.

Goodwill and the Nonprofit's Volunteer Programs

Perceptions and Behavior That Could Damage the Organization's Goodwill

Volunteer behavior and attitudes can shape perceptions or beliefs about the organization. Consider how the major donors of the Little Town Arts Festival must have felt when a volunteer in dirty blue jeans and a smelly T-shirt greeted them at the fund-raising event. The volunteer had the guest list in hand and was checking off the names of the donors as they entered. Board members attending the same event presented a stark contrast in their business attire. It was as if the management of the festival had neglected to tell the volunteer that the event was an important fundraiser. The volunteer in his grubby attire sent the message that he and the festival management didn't care how major donors were greeted—dirty work clothes would suffice. The donors were expected to make sizable pledges during the course of the evening but at the end of the evening the pledges simply didn't materialize. The major donors seemed to have received the unspoken message loud and clear.

Here are some other perceptions that could damage the reputation of the organization:

❑ discrimination in the selection/recruitment of volunteers,

❑ volunteers who don't know what they are doing,

❑ volunteers who are unsupervised/undisciplined, or

❑ volunteers who help themselves to resources that are intended to benefit the organization's clients.

Discrimination in the Selection/Recruitment of Volunteers

Volunteer staff members don't enjoy the same legal protections enjoyed by paid employees. Generally speaking, a volunteer doesn't have standing to sue under federal and state civil rights laws, such as Title VII of the Civil Rights Act of 1964. However, the impression that your organization discriminates against members of a particular protected class in its volunteer recruitment and placement process could have serious repercussions. The volunteer may approach a member of the media and find an outlet for his or her complaint. Or the volunteer may spread the word among friends and colleagues in your applicant pool.

Volunteers Don't Know What They Are Doing

Volunteers' actions, and sometimes reactions, in difficult situations will establish a perception about their overall competence. Volunteers who are well-trained and understand what is expected from them will probably be able to handle challenging situations better than those volunteers who are unclear about their role or the organization's expectations.

Volunteers Are Unsupervised/Undisciplined

Do volunteers in your organization have supervisors: people that they *know* are there to supervise them? Do your volunteers accept supervision? Volunteers who have difficulty understanding their role within the program and in the larger organization can come across as "loose cannons." Individuals who observe this behavior—or worse yet—are on the receiving end of this behavior or attitude come to the conclusion that the organization chooses not to control its volunteer workforce.

Volunteers Appear to Help Themselves to Resources That Are Intended to Benefit the Organization's Clients

In the case of the West County Thrift Shop, volunteers saw nothing wrong with the practice of skimming the best of the donations for themselves. They may have justified the practice by paying for the items. However, the clients of the thrift shop never had a chance to even consider purchasing the more luxurious items, which, in essence, robbed the thrift shop of a reputation for classy selections that would have drawn a broader range of, and possibly more, clientele.

Other Volunteer Conduct That Could Threaten Goodwill

The way volunteers conduct themselves and the attitudes that they present can either reinforce the good image of the organization or introduce doubt about the quality of service that the organization provides. Here are some examples of behavior that could seriously damage the organization's goodwill:

■ *Reckless or Dangerous Driving*

How a volunteer drives, particularly if driving a vehicle with the nonprofit's name on it, can be a public relations disaster in the making. Screening volunteer drivers and requiring them to produce a valid driver's license and a department of motor vehicles (DMV) record that meets the nonprofit's specific criteria will help protect the nonprofit in the event a volunteer is driving his or her own vehicle on the organization's business, and potentially enable the nonprofit to spot unsuitable drivers before sending them on the road. Additionally, it's a good idea to schedule a safety briefing for volunteers who will be driving the organization's vehicles, or their own vehicles on behalf of the organization. The briefing should include a review of the organization's safe driving, vehicle maintenance and accident reporting policies.

■ *Arrogant or Irresponsible Personal Behavior While Representing the Organization*

The content of the volunteer orientation and the quality of supervision are essential to ensuring that all volunteers conduct themselves in a manner that will bring credit to the organization. Volunteers who work with clients or interact with donors and the public should be provided additional training in customer service and conflict resolution. Role-playing can be valuable in this type of training, as behaviors that would be problematic may be observed and experienced in the role-play. At that point, the behavior can be identified and redirected.

■ *Inappropriate Treatment of Others*

As part of the training for their assignment, volunteers should be informed that they have external and internal customers who will need volunteers' help and deserve to be treated with courtesy and respect. External customers include clients, donors and members of the public. Internal customers include members of the staff, management, board and other volunteers. Conflict management and problem-solving training, reinforced through "hands-on" exercises, may be effective ways to help volunteers refine their skills. Some volunteers may be new to the environment in which they will be working, so the training your volunteer program provides is especially helpful.

■ *When Volunteers Help Themselves to Resources Intended for Clients*

If this is a problem within your organization, then the volunteers need to be told immediately that this behavior is unacceptable. They should be trained from the time that they attend their first orientation that they aren't to take resources intended for clients. Then the message should be reinforced. There should also be consequences stated and enforced regarding this behavior.

- **Unauthorized Press Contact**

This behavior may occur when a volunteer program neglects to provide explicit instruction concerning its media relations policy. During the volunteer orientation, the organization should make it clear what its considers appropriate and inappropriate behavior. Volunteers need to understand that there is an official spokesperson for the organization and all questions from the media should be referred to that person, and, if that person is absent, to the executive director. The section in this chapter on handling crisis scenarios will provide additional recommendations.

- *Inappropriate Use of Technology*

Technological advances often bring new risks to the workplace. Before a volunteer is assigned computer access, he or she should have a thorough briefing on the nonprofit's technology policy, including issues related to equipment ownership, privacy, and restrictions on the use of the nonprofit's systems. As in other areas, supervision is key to ensuring that the organization's technology is used appropriately.

Risk Management Techniques in Volunteer Program Public Relations

One of the best ways of introducing issues around public relations is to build that component into the volunteer orientation. From the start of their partnership with the organization, volunteers, including board members, need to understand that to many observers, they *are* the organization. Maintaining public trust is essential for the organization to continue serving its clients and the community. If the nonprofit experiences erosion of public trust, then it will become difficult to raise money or work collaboratively with other nonprofits, government agencies or businesses. Ultimately, the clients will suffer because the services provided by the nonprofit might no longer be available.

As the topics of goodwill and public trust are raised in the volunteer orientation, emphasize what is good and appropriate behavior in all situations and in all interactions with internal and external customers. Discuss the mission and values of the organization and provide examples of how appropriate behavior can put these into action. It's important to illustrate appropriate and inappropriate behavior. Never assume that the distinction is intuitive for the volunteer staff. Some situations, particularly those involving customer service, can be sensitive. Taking extra time to review these situations and describe the organization's expectations is well worth the effort.

Holding routine "in-service" training is a way to reinforce the program's expectations for service delivery as well as behavior. Use these sessions to explain, perhaps citing recent incidents as examples, what *is* and *isn't* appropriate behavior and why.

Finally, the volunteer program's paid and unpaid staff need to understand the consequences of inappropriate behavior as well as the nonprofit's commitment to apply these consequences evenly and without regard to pay status.

The Intersection of Public Relations and Crisis Management

You are the executive director of the Sunnyside Child Care Center. You open up the morning paper to find that your organization has made the front page—above the fold. The headline reads:

"Board Chair of Sunnyside Children's Center Arrested for Trafficking in Kiddie Porn"

Crises can be triggered by many types of events including accidents, death or disability of a crucial person, destruction of the building housing the nonprofit, or the criminal behavior of board, staff or volunteers. The media reports of these events can cast a negative light on the nonprofit in the short run, but the way in which the crisis is handled determines the effect on the nonprofit in the long term.

Although not all crises are as shocking as the one in the sample headline, media reports can quickly bring negative attention to a nonprofit. Some examples include the mismanagement of funds, inappropriate behavior, wrongful termination, or injury to a client or a member of the public. The nature of some of these events, such as a traffic accident injuring clients or criminal behavior, will generate media attention. However, other types of crises, such as the termination of a staff member or the mismanagement of funds need not generate prolonged attention if handled properly.

Sometimes media attention can be generated over matters that appear benign. A nonprofit animal shelter received extensive media attention when word got out that it had recruited a new executive director from another city with a salary-and-benefits package that exceeded the compensation package of the governor of the state. The employment offer received attention in the print and broadcast media over a two-week period. As part of the coverage, the media reminded its audience that this animal shelter had a checkered past, which included allegations of financial mismanagement. The media also interviewed a number of city government officials, who each categorically condemned the size of the compensation package.

As with any risk management issue, the skillful handling of a crisis requires planning well in advance. In the following section we touch on some of these issues. For more information on crisis management, consider consulting: *Vital Signs: Anticipating, Preventing and Surviving a Crisis in a Nonprofit*, published by the Nonprofit Risk Management Center. Some of the key areas for planning include handling media inquiries, preparing volunteers for a crisis, and handling lower level crises.

Handling Media Inquiries

During certain types of crises, a representative of the media who is seeking the organization's response to the situation will contact a volunteer program. Every volunteer program should have an official spokesperson for media inquiries, and it's vital that *everyone* in the organization knows the identity of that spokesperson. Volunteers also need to know that they are to refer all media inquiries to this individual and *why* it is necessary to have only one person talking to the media.

When the media contacts the spokesperson, the individual needs to be truthful and report only factual data. Speculation is always inappropriate. If the spokesperson doesn't know the answer, he or she should say, "I don't know," and then offer to look into the matter and provide information at a later time. The spokesperson should *never* say anything to the media that he/she would not want to hear on television or read on the front page of the local newspaper. "Off the record" is *never* off the record.

Having a prepared statement ready is another method of dealing with press inquiries. Here is an example of a prepared statement:

> We are very aware of the recent allegations against a volunteer in our organization. Information regarding these allegations is confidential at this time and we are not permitted to discuss the case. However, we do wish to state that client safety has been and continues to be our top priority. We are working collaboratively with the authorities to get to the bottom of the allegations and get back to our core mission of serving residents of this community.

The prepared statement can be modified to fit the needs of the particular scenario, but the framework acknowledges that there is an allegation of wrongdoing, that the organization is committed to safety, and that the organization is cooperating with authorities to resolve the questions raised by the allegations.

Preparing Volunteers for a Crisis

As part of their training, tell volunteers what they are expected do in the event they are involved in a serious accident or other crisis situation. Volunteers should know:

❑ to whom they should refer media inquiries,

❑ whom they should call when they have an emergency,

❑ what they should do or *should not* do, and

❑ not to comment on responsibility for or cause of the incident.

For direct service volunteers it might be helpful to stage crisis simulations so that they can practice response skills. Having regular in-service training concerning the handling of emergencies will raise the awareness of your volunteers about the possibility of a crisis, and help them cope more effectively should an emergency arise.

Handling Lower Level Crises

Some crises don't begin as public matters, but have the potential to become very public and very nasty. For example, when a major donor received an unsolicited e-mail from one of the organization's volunteers, the donor sent back a simple directive: "Don't send me any more e-mail messages." The volunteer responded, calling the major donor a "monster." The donor forwarded the e-mail string to a member of the board, who sent it on to the executive director.

In order to mitigate the situation and prevent it from escalating to a crisis, the executive director could do the following:

❑ assure the volunteer that action will be taken;

❑ call the donor to apologize, explain that action will be taken to deal with the situation and prevent it from recurring;

❑ meet with the directors of volunteers and development and the volunteer who sent the e-mail;

- [ ] show the e-mail messages to the volunteer to verify whether or not the volunteer was the author;

- [ ] if the volunteer admits to sending the e-mail, explain how this behavior violates the nonprofit's code of conduct and then terminate the volunteer's service, or, if the volunteer claims that someone else sent the e-mail, investigate his or her claim; and

- [ ] instruct the information technology staff to suspend e-mail privileges for the volunteer until the executive director tells them to reinstate privileges for this user (when the volunteer is cleared.)

The executive director then needs to take steps to ensure that this won't happen again:

- [ ] Schedule a *mandatory* all-staff briefing on the use of e-mail in the agency, explaining how inappropriate or abusive e-mail can damage the organization's reputation and relationships with its stakeholders.

- [ ] Call both the donor and the board member who reported the incident and advise them of the actions taken.

- [ ] Consider sending the donor flowers, taking the donor to lunch or extending to the donor an invitation to a special event to make up for the unpleasantness.

Conclusion

Public trust and confidence are crucial to the survival of any nonprofit. In order to provide services for clients and the community, an organization needs to be free from harmful perceptions, doubts about the quality of service and negative publicity. Central to good public relations are routine discussions, training and planning. Taking a proactive approach to maintaining good public relations will help volunteers become more conscious of the effect of their actions, help the board members to understand the importance of their role, and ultimately benefit the nonprofit's clients by providing services in a safe, positive environment. Chapter 10 will discuss insuring volunteers as a further means of protecting the organization and its mission.

Chapter 10
Insurance for Volunteer Programs

I nsurance is one available technique for financing losses. Insurance doesn't prevent losses from occurring or safeguard participants, but it can provide a way to pay for insured losses and the cost associated with investigating or defending accidents or allegations of wrongdoing.

While a volunteer program considers what types of insurance might be appropriate, the organization's leaders should be thinking about the types of losses that may occur. One place to start is the following major categories of claims:

❏   claims filed *against the nonprofit* that result from harm or loss *suffered by* volunteer workers while providing service for the organization or loss *caused by* volunteers while performing service for the organization; and

❏   claims filed *against the volunteer* alleging harm caused by the volunteer while performing service for the organization.

Each category of claims suggests different insurance products and considerations. In this chapter, we will provide an overview of the options facing volunteer programs and a suggested approach to determining how an organization might insure these risks.

Claims Against the Nonprofit

Most nonprofits that engage volunteers in service projects are deeply concerned about the possibility that a volunteer worker will suffer an injury while performing a service. In certain types of organizations, the concern about volunteer injury is a top priority. Examples of such organizations are those sending volunteers to third world countries for emergency aid projects or U.S.-based projects where volunteers are involved in home building, outdoor activities, disaster response or work with difficult client populations. Within this category, potential claims can be further divided into two types:

❏ claims seeking payment of medical expenses for injuries suffered while volunteering; and

❏ claims seeking compensatory and/or punitive damages from the nonprofit for its negligence in supervising the activity or program in which the volunteer was injured.

Payment of Medical Expenses

The first group of claims may be insured in one of two ways. It's important to keep in mind, however, that the volunteer's existing health benefits coverage—through participation in an employer's, spouse's or self-employed program—will be primary (respond first) over any coverage provided by the nonprofit. Here are the options for covering medical expenses.

❏ **Volunteer Accident Policy**—Volunteer accident policies are relatively inexpensive policies that finance the cost of medical treatment for volunteers who are injured while delivering services for the organization. These policies usually pay the costs of emergency room services and follow-up treatment to predetermined limits based upon the kind of injury. An accident policy will not pay for an illness suffered by the volunteer, such as the flu, but it will respond if the illness is the result of an accident. Accident policies generally have a per accident limit ranging from $5,000 to $25,000 (higher limits are available) and an aggregate limit for either any one accident or for all claims paid during the policy year. Many policies have a sublimit for accidental loss of limbs or eyes.

One distinctive feature of an accident and injury policy is that it will pay a claim *regardless* of who is at fault. These policies are excess (versus primary) insurance, meaning that they pay only after other available insurance—generally the volunteer's personal health insurance—is exhausted, doesn't apply, or is subject to a deductible or co-payment provision. If the volunteer is uninsured, the accident and injury policy "drops down" and becomes primary coverage for the injury.

Since the coverage is written on an excess basis, accident policies are relatively inexpensive. Coverage can be purchased on a primary basis at a much higher cost.

❏ **Commercial General Liability Policy**—Most commercial general liability (CGL) policies include a section providing coverage for Medical Expenses. The typical CGL policy has a per person limit between $5,000 and $10,000. The coverage is similar to the accident policy in that it will pay if the injury arises from the nonprofit's operations or premises, regardless of who is at fault. One of the common exclusions under Medical Expense coverage is that the coverage does not apply to "any insured," including volunteers covered as "additional insureds." If volunteers are not insureds under your policy, the Medical Expense coverage would apply to any volunteer injury, subject to the terms of the policy. Some insurance companies allow nonprofits to extend Medical Expense coverage to volunteers, even when the volunteers are listed as insureds or additional insureds on the policy.

❏ **Workers' Compensation Policy**—Some states permit the inclusion of volunteers on a nonprofit's workers' compensation policy. A workers' compensation policy pays for medical expenses as well as lost wages resulting from a "work-related" injury. Therefore, if a volunteer is injured while "working" for the nonprofit, he or she might be eligible for workers' compensation benefits. Under the workers' compensation policy, the medical benefits are unlimited, unlike the Volunteer Accident or Medical Expense coverage under the commercial general liability policy, which limit medical benefits.

On the surface, this appears to be an easy answer to the dilemma of providing a source of recovery for injured volunteers. Workers' compensation is required for all employers in most states (in 14 states small employers whose staffs fall under a defined threshold are exempt from purchasing the otherwise compulsory coverage). Nonprofits are generally required to carry this coverage for their employees and it may be administratively less cumbersome to simply add volunteers to an existing policy.

Workers' compensation policies may not, however, be the most effective way for a nonprofit to protect its volunteers. WC policies for employees include a number of benefits for which volunteers wouldn't be eligible—reimbursement for lost wages, for example. In addition, WC premiums are based on position categories and total payroll, not the amount of time spent on the job. For example, the cost of insuring a patrol officer may be comparable to the cost of insuring a part-time police department volunteer who patrols a community as part of a crime deterrence effort. Another issue is how to determine the payment of lost wages if the injury results in

Workers' Compensation Resources

The U.S. Department of Labor maintains a list of State Workers' Compensation Laws at:

www.dol.gov/esa/regs/statutes/owcp/stwclaw/stwclaw.htm

For a comprehensive *Workers' Compensation Administrators Directory for the U.S. and Canada*, visit www.comp.state.nc.us/ncic/pages/wcadmdir.htm. The Directory was compiled by Robert W. McDowell for the North Carolina Industrial Commission, 4340 Mail Service Center, Raleigh, North Carolina 27699-4340.

The following Web site also offers valuable background information on workers' compensation coverage:

www.law.cornell.edu/topics/workers_compensation.html

time away from work. Will a doctor who performs home repair on a volunteer basis and suffers an injury be reimbursed for lost income as a doctor, or the average salary of a carpenter? In addition, actual losses under workers' compensation policies can dramatically affect future premiums. If losses paid for volunteer injuries exceed the premium paid by the nonprofit, the policy may be cancelled or a premium surcharge applied to future premiums. With a large volunteer workforce, accidents may occur and drive up the nonprofit's premium substantially.

One potential advantage to the nonprofit of using workers' compensation coverage is that the "exclusive remedy" doctrine applies to this type of coverage; therefore, the volunteer covered by WC may be precluded from pursuing a liability claim against the nonprofit. However, at least one state (Colorado) has ruled that a volunteer covered under workers' compensation can also file a liability claim against the nonprofit if the volunteer believes the nonprofit acted negligently.

Defense of Liability Claims Against the Nonprofit

What if an injured volunteer sues the volunteer program and alleges that his or her injuries resulted from negligence on the part of the nonprofit? What if a service recipient sues a nonprofit alleging negligence by a volunteer social worker or negligent driving by a volunteer coach? There are four possible coverages that might apply: commercial general liability, directors' and officers' liability, professional liability or automobile liability.

❑ **Commercial General Liability**—CGL policies protect a nonprofit and its directors, officers and employees against claims alleging property damage or bodily injury caused by the nonprofit's operations or activities. CGL policies generally offer broad coverage for damage to another's property, bodily injury, personal injury (false arrests, malicious prosecution, or defamation), and advertising injury (offenses arising from the nonprofit's advertising materials). Although a CGL policy provides broad coverage, it doesn't address every possible liability exposure. For instance, it doesn't deal with pollution, intentional injury, liquor liability, or use of an automobile. A CGL policy will pay the cost to defend against allegations that may be covered by the policy, as well as damages due to the insured's negligence. Some insurers are willing to extend the CGL policy to provide coverage for such others as volunteers, sponsors, funders and landlords.

If volunteers are identified as "additional insureds" under the policy, the policy will defend both the nonprofit and the volunteer in any covered claim. There are certain instances where the policy will *not* protect employees or volunteers individually, even though they are additional insureds. For example, no employee or volunteer is protected for bodily injury or personal injury to any fellow employee or any fellow volunteer, or the spouse, child, parent, brother or sister of another other employee or volunteer. Most CGL policies *do not* protect an employee or volunteer for property damage to property controlled by the nonprofit, the employee or volunteer, or any fellow employee or volunteer.

Although rare today, some CGL policies contain an exclusion for *any claim filed by one insured against another insured* (aptly called the "insured versus insured exclusion"). Therefore, if a volunteer attempted to file a claim against the nonprofit, the insurer would deny the claim since the policy does not cover one insured filing a claim against another insured. Most general liability policies today contain a severability clause that treats each insured as a *separate entity*. These more common policies do not exclude insured versus insured claims.

❏ **Directors' and Officers' Liability**—D&O policies protect against claims alleging harm attributable to the governance or management of an organization, with the exception of bodily injury or property damage. For example, when the volunteer board chair of a nonprofit angrily kicks a participant at a public event, the nonprofit's D&O carrier is likely to deny a claim filed in the aftermath of a suit filed by the victim. Generally, D&O policies don't list specific types of covered claims, but provide coverage for any "wrongful act."

A "wrongful act" may be an actual or alleged act, error or omission by the organization itself, or its directors, officers, employees and volunteers. A suit by a volunteer against a nonprofit might be precluded under the "insured versus insured" exclusion that is common on D&O policies. In most cases this exclusion is only removed with respect to employment claims. No "standard" D&O policy exists, so policy wording must be studied carefully to determine whether coverage applies in a particular instance.

Under most D&O policies, the insured parties include the nonprofit, its directors, officers, committee members, employees and volunteers working under the direction of the organization. Therefore, if volunteers are listed as insureds, the policy will protect the volunteer individually for any claims for wrongful acts, subject to the terms of the insurance contract. This coverage is especially important if the volunteer is a member of the board of directors or a committee.

❑ **Professional Liability**—A professional liability policy will protect the nonprofit for its errors and omissions in the delivery of professional services. Many professional liability policies sold to nonprofits specifically protect against allegations of negligence by employees or volunteers. For example, a legal aid society's lawyers' professional liability policy may cover both the nonprofit and the program's volunteer lawyers as "insureds." The professional liability claim would respond to allegations of malpractice by a volunteer lawyer. Most professional liability policies purchased by nonprofits don't specifically exclude volunteers as insureds, except when:

■ the policy covers specific professions, and there is no coverage for the volunteer's particular profession;

■ the policy requires that covered professionals be listed on the policy and the volunteer isn't listed;

■ the policy excludes unlicensed professionals and the particular volunteer no longer has an active license in his or her profession.

❏ **Automobile Liability**—A nonprofit can be held liable for an automobile accident for vehicles it owns, rents, hires, borrows or leases. The exposure also extends to vehicles owned by employees and volunteers that are used while performing service for the organization. Under an automobile liability policy, an insured includes anyone using a covered auto that the named insured owns, hires or borrows with the named insured's permission. Therefore, a volunteer is an insured when driving a vehicle owned, hired or borrowed by the nonprofit. However, insured status is not extended to the owner of any hired or borrowed auto or to employees when using *their own* vehicles. Another exception is that since the extension only applies to autos owned, hired or borrowed by the nonprofit, a nonowned vehicle does not meet the insured criteria. Nonowned autos include any vehicle owned by an employee or members of the employee's household. Therefore, volunteers are not insureds under a nonprofit's auto policy when driving their own vehicles. The volunteer's personal auto insurance would respond first to any auto loss. A nonprofit can purchase Hired and Nonowned Auto Liability coverage that will respond after the volunteer's personal auto coverage has been exhausted. The volunteer's personal auto liability policy will also protect the nonprofit.

Claims Against the Volunteer

Fear of incurring personal liability for volunteer service in isn't uncommon among the estimated 90 million Americans who perform volunteer service each year. Volunteer board members may be targeted in suits alleging wrongful employment practices, breach of fiduciary duty, fraud and other causes of action. Suits against volunteer service providers may allege negligence or gross negligence in caring for a client. Despite the relative infrequency of these actions, it's important to understand the legal and insurance protections available to your volunteers.

There are two major categories of protection that a volunteer can turn to if he or she faces a suit: volunteer protection laws at the state and federal levels, and insurance. The first category will be addressed in Chapter 10. We now turn our attention to the insurance options.

It's important to keep in mind that many nonprofits purchase broad forms of coverage that will defend a volunteer should he or she be named in a suit (These four coverages were discussed in the prior section). And in some cases, an insurer may elect to defend a volunteer even if the coverage was intended to protect the nonprofit only. If volunteers aren't covered as insureds under the nonprofit's CGL, D&O or professional liability policies or the nonprofit doesn't purchase any coverage, the volunteer may look to his personal homeowners' policy or renters' policy for coverage. Other options are a volunteer liability policy purchased by the nonprofit to provide additional protection for its volunteers, and the volunteers' personal auto liability policies.

❑ **Homeowners' or Renters' Policies**—Volunteers who are homeowners may enjoy some protection under their existing homeowners' policies. In some cases coverage is provided for volunteer activities without the need for any action on the part of the homeowner. In other instances the homeowner must request a broadening endorsement to cover his or her volunteer activities. Whether the endorsement is provided at no additional cost or minimal cost, this coverage is potentially valuable protection in the event the volunteer is named in a suit. Volunteers who have a renters' policy may enjoy similar protection.

It's important to keep in mind, however, that many homeowners' and renters' policies don't cover losses stemming from alleged "wrongful acts." They are limited to damages from bodily injury or property damage. Some policies include personal injury (libel, slander, defamation, invasion of privacy, etc.). Consequently, some homeowners' policies will only pay for the homeowner's negligent acts that result in bodily injury or damage to the property of others—and won't respond if the homeowner is accused of violating someone's civil rights (e.g. in an employment practices suit) or mismanaging the organization (e.g. a suit alleging fraud by the board) while volunteering.

Since these policies differ to a large extent, urge your nonprofit's volunteers to check their policies and discuss their board or other volunteer service with their insurance agent to determine the extent to which their homeowner's or renter's policy provides coverage.

❑ **Volunteer Liability Policies**—It's likely that a significant percentage of Americans who volunteer don't have the option of relying on a homeowners' or renters' policy for coverage simply because they don't purchase such policies. Another option is available in the form of a Volunteer Liability Policy, a type of personal liability coverage. This coverage is typically packaged with a Volunteer Accident policy that is purchased by a nonprofit. For example, one provider offers up to $1 million in personal liability insurance and up to $500,000 in excess automobile liability insurance above the volunteer's own insurance as part of its volunteer insurance package. The personal liability coverage provides protection for a personal injury or property damage liability claim arising out of the volunteer's duties on behalf of the nonprofit. Exclusions include alleged errors or omissions in connection with the volunteer's professional services and property damage to property in the care, custody or control of the volunteer. In some cases, a state agency or state-sponsored insurance program may offer volunteer coverage at a reasonable cost.

❑ **Personal Auto Liability Policies**—A volunteer who will be driving his or her auto while providing service for a nonprofit should review his or her personal auto coverage. For a board member, the service might involve attending a board meeting or other of the nonprofit's events and activities. For other volunteers the service performed could involve transporting clients or running errands. The volunteer's personal auto policy will extend protection to the nonprofit while the volunteer is driving for the nonprofit.

Most states have laws that require the owner of a motor vehicle to purchase minimum levels of liability insurance. Volunteers should review their policy limits and consider the need to increase these limits depending on the nature of the services they provide to a nonprofit.

Conclusion

A partnership between the nonprofit and its insurance professional is the way to attain the most satisfactory coverage. The nonprofit is in the best position to identify its risks and rank them in priority order (from the most likely and most to the least likely to occur). The insurance professional can undertake the leg work required to identify the most appropriate coverage for the nonprofit at a price the organization can afford.

Chapter 11
Volunteer Protection Laws

G ood Samaritan Laws. Volunteer Protection. Volunteer
Immunity. Liability Limitation. Shield Laws. Charitable
Immunity. These terms, which have significant, as well as
subtle distinctions, are used to describe laws that protect people
and organizations in the nonprofit sector from claims, lawsuits
and allegations of wrongdoing. Although many researchers,
legal authorities and other interested persons have written
about these subjects during the past 20 years, a tremendous
degree of confusion remains about whether volunteers can be
sued and found liable for negligent acts. The question on the
mind of many volunteers is even more specific: "Could I lose
my house if someone gets hurt while I'm working at the food
pantry/coaching soccer/lending a hand at the homeless shelter
one weekend?" Nonprofit organizations owe it to themselves to
understand what, if any, protection is available from federal or
state law.

The Volunteer Protection Act of 1997

In the late 1980s several federal legislators began proposing
ways to remove the liability chill from volunteering. Rep. John
Porter (R-Ill.) dramatized the problem by assigning bill number
911 to his proposed Volunteer Protection Act. In 1990, President
George H.W. Bush released a model act and called for the state-
by-state adoption of volunteer protection legislation. In

response to growing concern about liability, state legislatures began taking action.

In 1997, Congress—with the purpose of encouraging people to volunteer their services while seeking to ease fears of volunteer liability—passed the federal Volunteer Protection Act [42 U.S.C. § 14503(a)]. At the time the VPA was adopted, every state had a law limiting the liability of certain volunteers.

The final version of the Volunteer Protection Act—signed into law by President Bill Clinton on June 18, 1997—preempts state laws "to the extent that such laws are inconsistent with the Act."

"Generally speaking, the VPA provides immunity from lawsuits filed against a nonprofit's volunteer where the claim is that he carelessly injured another in the course of helping the nonprofit. The act does not provide immunity to the organization itself" [source: www.npccny.org].

However, the VPA doesn't take precedence over a state law that provides additional protection from liability for volunteers. Nor does the VPA pre-empt state law with respect to a number of conditions that may be incorporated in state law.

These conditions include:

a. that a nonprofit adhere to risk management procedures, including mandatory training of volunteers;

b. laws that make a nonprofit liable for the acts or omissions of its volunteers to the same extent that an employer is liable for the acts or omissions of its employees;

c. provisions that render the immunity inapplicable if an officer of a state or local government brought the civil action; and

d. provisions that limit the applicability of immunity to nonprofits that provide a "financially secure source of recovery," such as insurance.

In addition, the federal law's protections don't apply to civil actions in which all parties are citizens of the state that has enacted a statute declaring that the VPA doesn't apply.

Simply stated, the Volunteer Protection Act provides immunity for volunteers serving nonprofit organizations* or governmental entities for harm caused by their acts or omissions if:

❏ *the volunteer was acting within the scope of his or her responsibilities at the time of the alleged act or omission.* Unfortunately, in many cases the scope of a volunteer's responsibility isn't defined. In some cases a volunteer will take it upon him or herself to undertake service for the organization.

❏ *appropriate or required, the volunteer was properly licensed, certified or authorized to act.* Whether it was appropriate for a volunteer to be authorized to act will not be readily apparent in all instances.

❏ *the harm was not caused by willful, criminal or reckless misconduct, gross negligence or a conscious, flagrant indifference to the rights or safety of the individual harmed.* Some commentators have argued that this condition provides guidance to plaintiff's counsel in terms of wording a complaint so that it will avoid the protection of the VPA. A plaintiff need only state that a volunteer's action was willful or in flagrant indifference to the rights and safety of the individual harmed for the matter to require a factual determination by a court. In these cases, the volunteer may be unable to escape the suit on a motion for summary judgment and must defend him or herself.

❏ *the harm was not caused by the volunteer operating a motor vehicle, vessel, or aircraft where the state requires an operator's license and insurance.*

*Unlike most state volunteer protection laws, the federal law does not require that a nonprofit qualify as a tax-exempt organization in order for its volunteers to enjoy protection.

The VPA may dissuade some individuals and organizations from suing volunteers. In addition, it provides a defense for volunteers facing liability suits. Nevertheless, despite the VPA, many volunteers remain *fully liable* for any harm they cause, and all volunteers remain liable for some actions. The law only protects volunteers serving certain nonprofits and governmental entities (See www.nonprofitrisk.org - *State Liability Laws for Charitable Organizations and Volunteers — 4th Edition*). In addition, the VPA doesn't prevent a nonprofit from bringing an action against a volunteer.

State Volunteer Protection Laws

Every state in the United States has a law that pertains specifically to the legal liability of *some* volunteers. These laws differ to a great extent. Some state volunteer protection laws only protect directors and officers serving nonprofits; others protect narrow categories of volunteers, such as firefighters or other emergency service personnel.

In several cases state legislatures have added new wording to their volunteer protection laws that clarifies or expands the protection previously afforded or represents an attempt to adjust the law so it's consistent with the federal Volunteer Protection Act. There continues to be a wide range of exceptions to the protections afforded under these laws, as well as other differences reflecting the preferences or specific concerns of individual state legislatures.

Exceptions to Liability Protection: Common and Unusual

It's arguable that the exceptions to the protections provided by the state statutes serve to eliminate protection for volunteers in a great number—perhaps even the majority—of the actual claims filed against nonprofit volunteers. The most common exceptions contained in the various state statutes include:

1. eliminating the protection for volunteer conduct found to be willful or wanton;

2. gross negligence on the part of the volunteer; and

3. wrongful acts committed while operating a motor vehicle.

Ironically, the third exception noted accounts for a large number of claims filed against volunteers, yet the protection is denied by statute in many states. On a practical level, the first two exceptions serve to reduce (but not eliminate) the possibility that a suit against a volunteer will be dismissed on summary judgment.

Additional, yet less common exceptions featured in the state laws include:

4. the exception for fraud or fiduciary misconduct;

5. the exception for actions brought by an attorney general or other state official;

6. the exception for the delivery of certain professional services; and

7. the exception for knowing violations of the law.

Conditions May be Required

In addition to specified exceptions, there are recurring requirements to be met for the limitation on liability to apply. Examples of the conditions that attach to various volunteer protection laws include the requirement that:

❏ the nonprofit retaining the volunteer carry liability insurance at a specified level.

❏ the nonprofit amend its articles of incorporation or bylaws to specifically indemnify volunteers.

❏ certain volunteers receive training from the nonprofit.

❏ volunteers receive prior written authorization in order to act on behalf of the nonprofit.

The conditions described above are consistent with the federal law's intent: to ensure that the nonprofit, not the volunteer serving the nonprofit, is financially responsible for negligent acts or omissions committed by an uncompensated volunteer. However, there is often great irony in these conditions. For example, the insurance requirement often means that volunteers serving the smallest nonprofits—those with only meager resources—often don't enjoy any protection under the state volunteer protection law, while those volunteering for larger organizations, which can afford liability insurance, will enjoy protection.

The three other conditions lead to a similar Catch-22 outcome: volunteers who are serving smaller, more informal organizations face the greatest exposure, because the lack of sophistication and resources of the nonprofits they serve removes the protection the volunteers would otherwise enjoy under the state volunteer protection law.

Unusual Provisions May be Included

There are a number of unusual provisions noted in a state-by-state review of the volunteer protection laws. For example:

❑ In Arkansas, volunteers lose the shelter of the volunteer protection statute if they are covered by liability insurance. Where this is the case, the volunteer's liability for simple negligence is limited to the liability limit of the applicable insurance policy.

❑ In Colorado, a section of the code immunizes, "all bingo-raffle volunteers...from civil actions and liabilities if they acted in good faith and within the scope of their official duty for a charitable organization."

❑ The Delaware volunteer protection law specifically defines "organization" as any "not-for-profit organization exempt from federal income tax under § 501(c) of the Internal Revenue Code." Several other state laws limit protection to nonprofits that have obtained federal tax-exempt status.

❑ The Hawaii volunteer protection act shields volunteers serving nonprofits that carry liability insurance with an aggregate limit of $500,000 or that have annual revenues of less than $50,000. Ironically, this statute leaves unprotected a potentially large group of volunteers—persons volunteering for nonprofits with budgets larger than $50,000, but that still can't afford liability coverage.

❏ Ohio's volunteer protection law pertaining to athletic program volunteers only applies if at the time of the act or omission the athletic coach or trainer had completed a requisite safety course.

❏ In South Dakota, a separate statute provides that to the extent any volunteer, nonprofit corporation or organization, governmental entity or charitable hospital participates in a risk-sharing pool or purchases liability insurance, the immunity provided by the state's volunteer protection law (§ 47-23-29) is waived and can't be raised as an affirmative defense in court.

❏ In Vermont, *201 V.S. § 5781* provides that "a volunteer for a library will not be held personally liable for damages resulting from services provided to patrons in the course of duty or for information contained in library materials." Vermont's code also protects volunteers who administer rabies inoculations.

❏ Virginia's code contains numerous unusual provisions, including a provision protecting, "Any person who provides emergency obstetrical care to a woman in active labor who had not previously cared for her in connection with the pregnancy and did not have the woman's medical records readily available." Another section of the code protects "any person who in good faith and without compensation administers epinephrine to a person for whom an insect sting treatment kit was prescribed, if it is reasonably believed the person is about to suffer an anaphylactic reaction."

❏ In Wisconsin, a volunteer who provides services without compensation on behalf of the Roman

Catholic Church isn't liable to any person for any monetary liabilities arising from an act or omission as a volunteer. A separate provision indicates that a volunteer for a religious organization who provides services without compensation isn't liable to any person for any monetary liabilities arising from an act or omission as a volunteer.

Recent Case Law

A search for state-level cases citing the Volunteer Protection Act turns up a handful of cases. What follows is the discussion of the rulings and facts of two cases—one citing the federal law and one citing a state immunity law—in an effort to illustrate the application of volunteer protection laws in actual litigation against volunteers. It is important to keep in mind that these cases are state-level decisions that may be influential, but are not precedent-setting in other jurisdictions.

In *Trinkaus v. Mohawk Mountain Ski Area* (2003 WL 21304676), an injured skier sought compensation for personal injuries he suffered as a result of a 2001 skiing accident. The accident occurred when a young snowboarder collided with the plaintiff on the slopes. The snowboarder was attending a ski trip sponsored by a local Boy Scout troop. Defendants included the ski area, the troop's scoutmaster, two assistant scoutmasters, and the young scout causing the plaintiff's injury. Both the troop and its leaders filed motions for summary judgment. The Superior Court of Connecticut denied the troop's motion, which was based on its assertion that the troop owed no duty of care to the plaintiff. The court wrote, "This case presents circumstances in which the existence of a duty involves a mixed question of law and fact." The court, however, granted the scoutmaster's and assistant scoutmasters' motions for summary judgment pursuant to the Volunteer Protection Act. The dismissal of the case against the troop volunteers effectively precluded the need to determine whether these volunteers had, as the plaintiff alleged, "negligently entrusted a dangerous instrumentality" to the snowboarder.

In an appellate case from the District Court of Appeal of Florida, Fourth District, the court reversed a circuit court's order granting summary judgment to the estate of a volunteer, Ruben Berger, whose car rear-ended a female motorist. In *Campbell v. Kessler* (848 So.2d 369), the woman brought a suit alleging negligence by Berger who rear-ended her car in Boynton Beach, FL. At the time of the accident, Berger was driving a citizen patrol car that was owned by the local sheriff's office, as a volunteer member of a Citizen Observer Patrol. The trial court based its summary judgment ruling on section 768.1355(1) of the Florida Volunteer Protection Act. Florida is among the states whose volunteer protection laws do not exclude claims alleging negligence in the operation of a motor vehicle. In reversing the lower court ruling, the appellate court wrote that "There are substantial questions of material fact as to whether Berger acted as an ordinarily prudent person would have acted under the same or similar circumstances." In its ruling the court also indicated that a simple determination that the volunteer was acting within the scope of his duties was not sufficient to find protection under the Florida statute.

Frequently Asked Questions About the *Volunteer Protection Act*

Does the Volunteer Protection Act protect everyone working in a "volunteer" capacity? Do volunteers who receive a modest stipend enjoy protection under the law?

The VPA specifically protects a volunteer who: (1) performs services (including officers, directors, trustees and direct service volunteers); (2) volunteers for a nonprofit organization or governmental entity; and (3) either (a) receives no compensation (although reasonable reimbursement for expenses incurred is allowed), or (b) does not receive anything of value in lieu of compensation in excess of $500 per year.

Therefore, volunteers who don't meet these conditions enjoy no protection under the VPA. For example, someone working as a volunteer for an organization that isn't a nonprofit under the laws of the state in which it operates— such as a new organization that has yet to incorporate as a nonprofit—would arguably not be protected by the law. A volunteer who receives a stipend of $50 per month, or $600 annually, isn't protected under the VPA.

Does the VPA protect volunteers in the most common cases filed against nonprofits and volunteers?

No. Because most lawsuits against volunteers are employment disputes, the exclusion of suits alleging violation of state and federal civil rights laws serves to eliminate from coverage most—if not all—of the suits brought against volunteer board members. Another common source of claims stems from automobile accidents in which a volunteer was driving. The VPA doesn't (although some state laws may) protect volunteers under these circumstances.

Are there any potential negative consequences of federal volunteer protection?

There are several troubling consequences of the Volunteer Protection Act, including:

❏ Volunteers through nonprofit organizations often serve highly vulnerable populations. With a lessened fear of being held liable except for wanton or criminal acts, organizations may become complacent about screening, training and supervising volunteer staff, and volunteers may act inappropriately. Volunteers, also, may be more likely to take unacceptable risks or accept assignments and responsibilities for which they haven't received training. In addition, volunteers may not take their heightened duty of care for vulnerable populations seriously and, over time, feel less accountable for their actions.

❏ The VPA may reduce interest in and emphasis on risk management and safety programs over time. Risk management provides a means of protecting clients from harm, safely administering volunteer programs and preventing injuries. In many respects, the fear of liability has been an effective motivator for organizations to provide position descriptions, screening, training and supervision to paid and volunteer staff and to practice good risk management.

❑ The current tort system provides incentives for volunteers (and others) to exercise appropriate and reasonable care. Most U.S. citizens expect the people to whom they have entrusted the care of their children, elderly parents and others to exercise care in performing their duties.

❑ The VPA—and the state volunteer protection laws — have created the false impression that volunteers are immune from lawsuits. The federal Volunteer Protection Act added fuel to existing misconceptions about immunity and caused some to ignore the continuing possibility of suits against nonprofits and their volunteers. Many volunteers remain *fully liable* for any harm they cause, and all volunteers remain liable for some actions.

Conclusion

Determining whether a nonprofit will be liable for harm resulting from its acts or omissions depends on the confluence of various factors, including whether:

❑ the nonprofit had a duty of care with respect to those who were harmed,

❑ the nonprofit breached its duty of care,

❑ harm actually occurred,

❑ the harm that occurred was foreseeable,

❑ the breach of the duty of care was a proximate cause of harm that occurred, and

❑ there were reasonable measures available to the nonprofits that would have prevented the harm from occurring.

All of these considerations will be factored with the laws of a particular jurisdiction and the perspective and biases of the judge or jury who will consider the facts in a particular case. In so many instances, it is difficult, if not impossible, to predict whether liability will be imposed. Legal counsel representing the nonprofit, with full knowledge of all of the circumstances and facts at hand, will try to make this prediction and advise the nonprofit accordingly.

Bibliography

Carpenter, Clint, "Interviewing Volunteers: Being careful in the selection process," *The Nonprofit Times*, Feb. 15, 2000.

Culp, Ken III and Michael Nolan, "Trends That Will Impact Not-For-Profits For The Next 10 Years," *The Not-For-Profit CEO monthly letter*, Vol. 8, No. 10, August 2001, pages 1-3.

Delta Society, The Human-Animal Health Connection, www.deltasoiety.org.

Ellis, Susan J., "Service Intensity: Scaling options for volunteering," *The NonProfit Times*, Sept. 1, 2001, pages 28, 40.

Engaging Youth in Lifelong Service, Independent Sector and the Youth Service Alliance, Washington, D.C., 2002. (To order, visit www.independentsector.org.)

Experience at Work: Volunteering and Giving Among Americans 50 and Over, Independent Sector and AARP, Washington, D.C., 2003. (To order, visit www.independentsector.org.)

Kidding Around: A Guide to Safe Service Opportunities for Youth, Nonprofit Risk Management Center, Washington, D.C., 1996.

Merrill, Mary, "Risk Management," *Volunteer Literacy Manual*, Reading Recovery Council of North America, www.readingrecovery.org

Tremper, Charles and Gwynne Kostin, *No Surprises: controlling risks in volunteer programs*, Nonprofit Risk Management Center, Washington, D.C., 1993, out of print.

Your Guide to Youth Board Involvement and the Law, Youth on Board, Washington, D.C., 2001, www.youthonboard.org.

Resources

Watershed Support Program—*Working with Volunteers*, http://www.4sos.org/wssupport/group_support/volunteer.asp.

Journals and Newspapers

The Chronicle of Philanthropy - www.philanthropy.com

Nonprofit and Voluntary Sector Quarterly - http://nvs.sagepub.com

The NonProfit Times - www.nptimes.com

Free Management Library - www.managementhelp.org

The Electronic Gazette for Volunteerism - www.volunteertoday.com

Organizations

CompassPoint Nonprofit Services
731 Market Street, Suite 200
San Francisco, CA 94103
Telephone: (415) 541-9000; Fax: (415) 541-7708
www.compasspoint.org

Independent Sector
1200 Eighteenth Street, NW
Suite 200
Washington, DC 20036
Telephone: (202) 467-6100; Fax: (202) 467-6101
www.independentsector.org

BoardSource
1828 L Street, NW
Suite 900
Washington, DC 20036-5114
Telephone: (202) 452-6262 or (877) 892-6273
Fax: (202) 452-6299
www.boardsource.org

National Council of Nonprofit Associations
1030 15th Street, NW
Suite 870
Washington, DC 20005
Telephone: (202) 962-0322; Fax: (202) 962-0321
www.ncna.org

Nonprofit Risk Management Center
1130 Seventeenth Street, NW
Suite 210
Washington, DC 20036
Telephone: (202) 785-3891; Fax: (202) 296-0349
www.nonprofitrisk.org

The Points of Light Foundation
1400 I Street, NW
Suite 800
Washington, DC 20005-6526
Telephone: (202) 729-8000
www.pointsoflight.org

United Way of America
701 N. Fairfax Street
Alexandria, VA 22341
Telephone: (703) 836-7100
www.national.unitedway.org

Volunteer Consulting Group
6 E. 69th Street, Suite 602
New York, NY 10016
Phone: (212) 447-1236; Fax: (212) 447-0925
www.vcg.org

Online Resources
ARCH National Respite Network and Resource Center
www.archrespite.org/ARCHserv.htm

California Association of Nonprofits
www.canonprofits.org

Center for Non-Profit Corporations
www.njnonprofits.org

Corporation for National & Community Service, The Resource
Center, Effective Preactices Collection, Developing a Volunteer
Program
http://nationalserviceresources.org/epicenter/practices/
index.php?ep_action=viewtep_id=779

Council of Community Services of New York State, Inc.,
www.ccsnys.org

Colorado DOVIA – Directors of Volunteers in Agencies
List of resource links
www.dovia.org/

Delaware Association of Nonprofit Agencies
www.delawarenonprofit.org

Energize Inc.
www.energizeinc.com

Georgia Center for Nonprofits
www.gcn.org

Idealist.org, The Nonprofit FAQ
http://www.nonprofit-info.org/npofaq/16/00.html

Maine Association of Nonprofits
www.nonprofitmaine.org

Michigan Nonprofit Association
www.mnaonline.org

Minnesota Council of Nonprofits
www.mncn.org

Nonprofit Resource Center of Alabama
www.nrca.info

North Carolina Center *for* Nonprofits
www.ncnonprofits.org

University of Wisconsin Extension Program
Learner Resource Center, Nonprofit Management Educational
Resources
http://www.uwex.edu/learner/sites.htm

State Government Web Sites:

Check your own state government Web site for resources. The
following state Web sites have good resources.

Volunteer NH!—New Hampshire's Resource on Volunteerism
www.volunteernh.org/text/aboutover.htm

VirginiaService
www.vaservice.org

Other Publications From the Nonprofit Risk Management Center

A Golden Opportunity, Managing the Risks of Service to Seniors,
2003, ISBN 1-893210-12-X, 92 pages, $20.

Hauge, Jennifer Chandler and Melanie L. Herman, *Taking the
High Road, A Guide to Effective and Legal Employment Practices for
Nonprofits,* 2006, ISBN 1-893210-21-9, 225 pages, print and online
editions available, $45.

Herman, Melanie L. et al, *Coverage, Claims & Consequences: An
Insurance Handbook for Nonprofits,* 2002, ISBN 1-893210-11-1, 218
pages, $25.

Herman, Melanie L., *Pillars of Accountability, A Risk Management Guide for Nonprofit Boards,* 2006, ISBN 1-893210-22-7, 74 pages, $12.

Herman, Melanie L., *Ready in Defense: A Liability, Litigation and Legal Guide for Nonprofits,* 2003, ISBN 1-893210-13-8, 109 pages, $20.

Herman, Melanie L. and Barbara B. Oliver, *Vital Signs, Anticipating, Preventing and Surviving a Crisis in a Nonprofit,* 2001, ISBN 1-893210-06-5, 81 pages, $20.

Herman, Melanie L., and Dennis M. Kirschbaum, *No Strings Attached, Untangling the Risks of Fundraising & Collaboration,* 1999, ISBN 1-893210-04-9, 95 pages, $15.

Herman, Melanie L., *Full Speed Ahead: Managing Technology Risks in the Nonprofit World,* 2001, ISBN 1-893210-07-3, 120 pages, $25.

Mair, David L. and Melanie L. Herman, *Playing to Win: A Risk Management Guide for Nonprofit Youth Sports Programs,* 2003, 89 pages, $20.

Oliver, Barbara B., *Managing Facility Risks, 10 Steps to Safety,* 2004, ISBN 1-893219-16-2, 121 pages, $15.

Patterson, John C., *Staff Screening Tool Kit,* 2004, 3rd edition, ISBN 1-893210-18-9, 137 pages, $30.

Books on Volunteer Responsibilities and Management

Ellis, Susan J., *Focus on Volunteering KOPYKIT™: Ready-to-print Resources for Volunteer Organizations,* 2nd edition, Energize Books, 1999.

Ellis, Susan J., *From the Top Down: The Executive Role in Volunteer Program Success,* Energize Books, 1996.

Hughes, Sandra R., Berit M.Lakey and Marla J. Bobowick, *The Board Building Cycle: Nine Steps to Finding, Recruiting, and Engaging Nonprofit Board Members* (With CD-ROM), BoardSource, 2000.

Lee, Jarene Frances with Julia M. Catagnus, *What We Learned (The Hard Way) About Supervising Volunteers: An Action Guide to Making Your Job Easier,* Energize Books—Collective Wisdom Series, 1998.

Leifer, Jacqueline C. and Michael B. Glomb. *Legal Obligations of Nonprofit Boards: A Guidebook for Board Members*, Revised, BoardSource, 1997.

Ingram, Richard, *Ten Basic Responsibilities of Nonprofit Boards Kit*, BoardSource, 1997.

Presenting: Board Orientation (CD-Rom and User's Guide), An Introductory Presentation for Nonprofit Board Members, BoardSource, 2001.

NOTES

NOTES